IN ANL
TAM O' S_ _ER

The Story of a Tale

James Thomson

This edition of
In and Out of Tam o' Shanter
The Story of a Tale
ISBN 978-0-9566316-0-2

Is limited to 1,500 copies

By

James Thomson

Published by
James Thomson
6 Glebe Court, Kilmarnock KA1 3BD
01563 534423 / thomsonjmt@aol.com
31.7.2010

Dedication

This book is dedicated to my wife Sheena who has been a 'Burns Widow' for more years than I can remember but accepts it all with good humour and still remains a lady.

Acknowledgements

During the months I spent researching and compiling this book I received assistance and encouragement from many sources and I would like to recognise the help given to me by some of those people.

Chris Rollie gave valuable assistance and direction in Kirkcudbrightshire regarding Adam Forrester and, when I had difficulties, he recruited his friend Keith Kirk to help out. I am also obliged to Keith. Robert Wilson of New Cumnock assisted in finding specific references and Betty Haining, Secretary, Dumfries Ladies Burns Club, provided the information relating to the competition.

John Skilling of Alloway gave up a considerable amount of his time and walked me all over the village on a wet Scottish winter's day without complaint. He is a gentleman who possesses a patience which is a stranger to me. He even bought the coffee.

To my good friends Jim Haslett, John Givens, Jim Gibson and Joe Kennedy for allowing me to bore them to tears during my anorak phase yet still prompting and encouraging me constantly.

I have to thank East Ayrshire Council, in particular William Stafford, Director of Neighbourhood Services, for facilitating my access to their manuscript copy of the poem.

I must also thank my family, Sheena, Susan, Raymond and Leanne, for their help, support and constant encouragement.

Lastly, my old friend Alexander Robertson Drain, better known to the world as Sanny, who is sadly no longer with us. Alex used to drag me off to Burns Suppers all over the West of Scotland, ostensibly to toast the lassies, but it was really to be his straight man.

He would seldom introduce any of the forty seven Burns poems he could recite, just tell a joke and then begin. More often than not I would be the butt of that joke. The point to all this is that because we were on the same bill we travelled together, and during these journeys, he would regale me with Tam o' Shanter stories. When I asked him where he got the information, there were two standard answers "I read it somewhere", or even more cryptically "I heard it down in Girvan." And so I began to trace the sources of these stories and on every occasion I found a documented reference which was the starting point for all that follows.

Introduction

The poem Tam o' Shanter was first published in the Edinburgh Magazine in March 1791 a month before it appeared in The Antiquities of Scotland by Francis Grose. It was something new for Burns in the poetical field, a narrative. He expressed this view writing to Alexander Cunningham on 23 January 1791 saying 'It is my first essay in the way of tales.'

The poem is now part of Scottish national culture, and is recited too many times to count every year during the season of Burns Suppers. There is even an annual competition held in Dumfries which is keenly contested for the best recitation.

Yet despite being as well known as a poem, the background, the actual tale that it tells and the associated stories are seldom known or understood by the millions who hear the poem every year. Indeed a number of "Readers" who recite it appear to have no perception of the tale they are telling. It is a poem learned by rote without any understanding of the complicated, involved and beautiful tale that is Tam o' Shanter. Quite often this is also accompanied by comic acting and, sometimes, even props. I have also heard it recited with interludes of song referring to the two great football teams of Glasgow.

On the other hand when done by those who are aware, like Jim Brown from New Cumnock, or Angus Middleton from West Kilbride, the poem can be an uplifting experience. The poem can come alive, with the listener being entranced by the adventures of Tam and carried along with the changing pace of the narrative. The poem becomes what it was meant to be. A tale. Robert Burns certainly thought Tam o' Shanter to be his greatest work, which Professor Thomas Crawford described as "A breathless narrative tour de force worthy of Chaucer himself."

What follows is not an academic study or a literary critique of the poem but an attempt to explain the tale and bring all the various pieces of information relating to the narrative together. The one thing that is asked of the reader of what follows is the understanding that Tam o' Shanter was created for an 18th century audience. When Burns produced his epic tale it was with the knowledge that all his readers would be intimate with witchcraft and the ways of the Devil. It is for them, not us, that the piece was written.

the story of a tale

Contents

The Poem

Tam o' Shanter. A Tale

'*Of Brownyis and of Bogillis full is this Buke*' Gawin Douglas

When chapman billies leave the street,
And drouthy neebors, neebors meet,
As market-days are wearing late,
An' folk begin to tak the gate;
While we sit bousing at the nappy,
Getting fou and unco happy,
We think na on the lang Scots miles,
Mosses, waters, slaps and styles,
That lie between us and our hame,
Where sits our sulky sullen dame,   10
Gathering her brows like gathering storm,
Nursing her wrath to keep it warm.

This truth fand honest *Tam o' Shanter*,
As he fae Ayr ae night did canter,
(Auld Ayr wham ne'er a town surpasses,
For honest men and bonny lasses.)

O Tam hadst thou but been sae wise,
As ta'en thy ain wife *Kate*'s advice!
She tauld the weel thou was a skellum,
A blethering, blustering, drunken blellum;   20
That frae November till October'
Ae market-day thou was nae sober;
That ilka melder wi' the miller,
Thou sat as long as thou had siller;
That every naig was ca'd a shoe on,
The smith and thee got roaring fou on;
That at the L——d's house, even on Sunday,
Thou drank wi' Kirkton Jean till Monday.
She prophesised that late or soon,
Thou would be found deep drown'd in Doon;   30

Or catch'd wi' warlocks in the mirk,
By *Alloway's* auld haunted kirk.

Ah, gentle dames! It gars me greet,
To think how mony counsels sweet,
How many lengthen'd sage advices,
The husband frae the wife despises!

But to our tale; Ae market-night,
Tam had got planted unco right;
Fast by an ingle, bleezing finely,
Wi' reaming swats that drank divinely;   40
And at his elbow, Souter *Johnny*,
His ancient, trusty, drouthy crony;
Tam lo'ed him like a vera brither;
They had been fou for weeks thegither,
The night drave on wae sangs and clatter;
And ay the ale was growing better:
The landlady and *Tam* grew gracious,
Wi' secret favours, sweet and precious;
The Souter tauld his queerest stories;
The landlord's laugh was ready chorus;   50
The storm without might rair and rustle,
Tam did na mind the storm a whistle.

Care, mad to see a man sae happy,
E'en drown'd himself amang the nappy:
As bees flee hame wi' lades o' treasure,
The minutes wing'd their way wi' pleasure:
Kings may be blest, but *Tam* was glorious,
O'er a' the ills o' life victorious.

But pleasures are like poppies spread,
You seize the flower, the bloom is shed;   60
Or like the snow flake falls in the river,
A moment white – then melts for ever;
Or like the borealis race,

3

That flit ere you can point their place;
Or like the rainbow's lovely form,
Evanishing amid the storm,-
Nae man can tether time nor tide;
The hour approaches *Tam* maun ride;
That hour, o' nights black arch the key-stane,
That dreary hour he mounts his beast in;   70
And sic a night he taks the road in,
As ne'er poor sinner was abroad in.

The wind blew as 'twad blawn its last;
The rattling showers rose on the blast;
The speedy gleams the darkness swallow'd:
Loud, deep and lang the thunder bellow'd:
That night, a child might understand,
The Deil had business on his hand.

Weel mounted on his grey mare *Meg*,
A better never lifted leg,   80
Tam skelpit on thro' dub and mire,
Despising wind, and rain, and fire;
Whiles holding fast his gude blue bonnet;
Whiles crooning o'er an auld Scots sonnet;
Whiles glowering round wi' prudent cares,
Lest bogles catch him unawares:
Kirk- Alloway was drawing nigh,
Where ghaists and houlets nightly cry.

By this time he was cross the ford,
Where in the snaw, the chapman smoor'd;   90
And past the birks and miekle stane,
Where drunken *Charlie* brak's neck-bane;
And thro' the whins and by the cairn,
Where hunters fand the murder'd bairn;
And near the thorn, aboon the well,
Where Mungo's mither hang'd hersel.
Before him Doon pours all his floods,

4

The doubling storm roars thro' the woods;
The lightnings flash from pole to pole;
Near and more near the thunders roll;   100
When, glimmering thro' the groaning trees,
Kirk-Alloway seems in a bleeze;
Thro' ilka bore the beams were glancing;
And loud resounded mirth and dancing. —-
Inspiring bold *John Barleycorn*!
What dangers thou canst make us scorn!
Wi' tippeny, we fear nae evil;
Wi' usquabae, we'll face the Devil!
The swats sae reamed in *Tammie's* noddle,
Fair play, he car'd na deils a boddle.   110
But *Maggie* stood right sair astonish'd,
Till, by the heel and hand admonish'd,
She ventured forward on the light;
And, vow! *Tam* saw an unco sight!
Warlocks and witches in a dance;
Nae cotillion brent new fae France,
But hornpipes, jigs, strathspeys and reels,
Put life and mettle in their heels,
A winnock-bunker in the east,
There sat Auld Nick in shape o'beast;   120
A towzie tyke, black, grim and large,
To gie them music was his charge;
He screw'd the pipes and gart them skirl,
Till roof and rafters a' did dirl. —-
Coffins stood round, like open presses,
That shaw'd the dead in their last dresses;
And by some devilish cantraip sleight
Each in its cauld hand held a light. —-
By which heroic *Tam* was able
To note upon the haly table,   130
A murderer's banes in gibbet airns;

5

Twa span lang, wee, unchristen'd bairns;
A thief, new cutted frae a rape,
Wi' his last gasp his gab did gape;
Five tomahawks, wi' blude red-rusted;
Five scymitars, wi' murder crusted;
A garter, which a babe had strangled;
A knife, a father's throat had mangled,
Whom his ain son o' life bereft,
The grey hairs yet stack to the heft;   140
Wi' mair o' horrible and awefu',
Which even to name would be unlawfu'.

As *Tammie* glowr'd amazed and curious,
The mirth and fun grew fast and furious:
The piper loud and louder blew;
The dancers quick and quicker flew;
They reel'd, they set, they cross'd they cleekit,
Till ilka carlin swat and reekit,
And coost her duddies to the wark,
And linket at it in her sark!   150

Now, *Tam*, O *Tam*! Had they been queans,
A' plump and strapping in their teens,
Their sarks instead o' creeshie flannen,
Been snaw white seventeen hunder linen!
Thir breeks o' mine, my only pair,
That ance were plush, o' gude blue hair,
I would hae gi'en them off my hurdies,
For ae blink o' the bonie burdies!

But wither'd beldams, auld and droll,
Rigwoodie hags wad spean a foal,   160
Lowping and flinging on a crummock,
I wonder didna turn thy stomach.

But *Tam* kend what was what fu' brawlie,
There was ae winsome wench and wawlie,

6

That night enlisted in the core,
(Lang after kend on Carrick shore;
For mony a beast to dead she shot,
And perish'd mony a bony boat,
And shook baith meikle corn and bear,
And kept the countryside in fear :)   170
Her cutty sark, o' Paisley harn,
That while a lassie she had worn,
In longitude tho' sorely scanty,
It was her best and she was vauntie, —-
Ah! Little kend thy reverend grannie,
That sark she coft for her wee Nannie,
Wi' twa pund Scots, ('twas a' her riches),
Wad ever grac'd a dance of witches!

But here my Muse her wing maun cour;
Sic flights are far beyond her power;   180
To sing how Nannie lap and flang,
(A souple jade she was, and strang),
And how *Tam* stood like ane bewitch'd,
And thought his very een enrich'd;
Even Satan glowr'd and fidg'd fu' fain,
And hotch'd and blew wi' might and main:
Till first ae caper, syne anither,
Tam tint his reason a' thegither,
And roars out, "Weel done, Cutty-sark!"
And in an instant all was dark;   190
And scarcely had he Maggie rallied,
When out the hellish legion sallied.

As bees biz out wi' angry fyke,
When plundering herds assail their byke;
As open pussie's mortal foes,
When, pop! She starts before their nose;
As eager runs the market-crowd,
When 'Catch the thief!' resounds aloud;

So Maggie runs the witches follow,
Wi' mony an eldritch skreech and hollow.   200

Ah, *Tam*! Ah, *Tam*! Thou'll get thy fairin!
In hell they'll roast thee like a herrin!
In vain thy *Kate* awaits thy comin!
Kate soon will be a woefu' woman!
Now, do thy speedy utmost, Meg,
And win the key-stane of the brig;
There at them thy tail may toss,
A running stream they dare na cross.
But ere the key-stane she could make,
The fient a tail she had to shake!   210
For Nannie, far before the rest,
Hard upon noble Maggie prest,
And flew at *Tam* wi' furious ettle;
But little wist she Maggie's mettle —-
Ae spring brought off her master hale,
But left behind her ain gray tail:
The carlin claught her by the rump,
And left poor Maggie scarce a stump.

Now, wha this tale o' truth shall read,
Ilk man and mother's son, take heed;   220
Whene'er to drink you are inclin'd,
Or cutty-sarks run in your mind,
Think, you may buy the joys o'er dear;
Remember Tam o' Shanter's mare.

the story of a tale

Bogles and Witches

'*Of Brownyis and of Bogillis full is this Buke*' are the words chosen as the epigraph to the tale. They were written by Gawin Douglas (c1474-1522), a Scottish Bishop who was also a translator. Douglas was a prolific writer in Scots, with his principal work being The Eneados (from which the quote is taken), with other works such as the poems King Hart and Palice of Honour. He was one of the first to distinguish between the *Inglis* and *Scottis,* and wrote only in the vernacular.

Burns had read and enjoyed the works of Douglas, as he indicates in a letter to Robert Cleghorn 'Thanks, many thanks, for my Gawin Douglas.' That this quote is chosen gives us the first indication of what the poem contains.

Burns undoubtedly learned of spirit creatures from Betty Davidson a widowed cousin of his Mother Agnes. Betty was given board and lodging in the Burns house at Alloway in return for helping about the house. In his letter to Dr Moore on 2 August 1787 Burns states " *I owed much to an old Maid of my Mother's, remarkable for her ignorance, credulity and superstition, - She had I suppose, the largest collection in the country of tales and songs concerning devils, ghosts, fairies, brownies, witches, warlocks, spunkies, kelpies, elf towers, dragons and other trumpery, - This cultivated the latent seeds of posey; but had so strong an effect on my imagination, that to this hour in my nocturnal rambles I sometimes keep a sharp look-out in suspicious places: and though nobody can be more sceptical in these matters than I, yet it often takes an effort of Philosophy to shake off these idle terrors.*"

Burns also grew up near to the ruins of Alloway's Auld Kirk, which was a shell, and was no doubt of assistance to the fertile imagination of a young Robin already conditioned to accept the supernatural by the stories of Betty Davidson.

Indeed, on one occasion a Highland bullock strayed into the kirk, where it got stuck. Being without food or water it went half-mad. A day or two later, a local woman happened to be passing the kirk when she looked through the window and saw a pair of horns accompanied by loud bellowing. She fled in terror, convinced that the Devil had taken over the Auld Kirk.

John Tennant farmed at Laigh Corton Farm, which neighboured Mount Oliphant, and at the time of the incident with the bullock, was involved in the removal of the creature from the kirk. During this process the bullock lost a horn, which was retained by the Tennant family as detailed below. John Tennant later moved to Glenconner Farm at Ochiltree and is mentioned with respect by Burns in the poem Epistle to James Tennant of Glenconner, addressed to his son James. Burns writes;

"My heart-warm love to guid auld Glen,
The ace an' wale of honest men:"

Mr James Tennant great-grandson of John Tennant (Guid Auld Glen) writes about the incident *"The origin of this grotesque poetic deceit* [Tam o' Shanter] *is as follows: When our great-grandfather was at Corton, Bridge of Doon, a Highland bullock went amissing from one or other of the neighbouring pastures, strayed into the Kirk Yard, passed into the Kirk, could nowhere be found, and went half mad with hunger. A day or so after, some woman body passing the Kirk looked in and was saluted with a fearful roar, and seeing a pair of huge horns projecting above the seats in which the animal had become entangled, she fled in terror and raised the alarm that the Deil was in the Kirk. My grandfather, who was a youngster of perhaps thirteen or fourteen, was curious to see his 'Majesty', and recognising in him as the missing bullock, gave the necessary information, and was present when the beast was extricated. Robert Burns was a boy of perhaps eight or ten, and hearing the terrible story of the Kirk being invaded by 'Clootie' had it fixed in his mind, and afterwards wove it into the story of 'Tam o' Shanter'. In taking 'Nick' out of the Kirk one of his horns was knocked off and was taken to Corton. When the family removed to Glenconner, the horn was brought with them, and was long used as a bolting tube for giving medicine to cattle. Many years after, the sexton and town-crier in Ochiltree (Peter Kennet) being in want of a horn for making the village proclamations, and for blowing through the village in the early morning to waken the villagers – clocks then being few – the old Alloway 'Clootie' horn was then given to him, fitted with a silver mouthpiece, and used for years to call up the villagers to their daily work."* 1

The horn was fitted with silver mountings and was later given to the Town Crier of Ochiltree for his official duties. It reverted back to the Tennant family and is still in existence today in the possession of Lord Glenconner, who became famous as "The man who bought Mustique". A photograph of the horn is reproduced in The Ayrshire Book of Burns Lore by A. M. Boyle. 2

The story of the bullock mistaken for the Devil spread throughout the district and would have reinforced Robert's opinion of Kirk Alloway as *"a place so well known to be a favourite haunt of the devil and the devil's friends and emissaries."* (Letter to Francis Grose June 1790).

While bogles and the like may be harmless superstition and stories to frighten children, witchcraft in Scotland at that time was an altogether different matter.

The idea of witchcraft is not universal in all societies, but it was widespread throughout Europe from the middle ages. The common element in all witchcraft is of a general evil power. This leads to acts of witchcraft being seen as evil and witches as evil people. Largely witches were thought of, principally by the church, as individuals who could visit harm on people or animals by using sorcery, a curse, an incantation or by power of will.

There was a difference between White and Black Witches. White Witches were concerned with the healing arts, finding lost objects and similar harmless pursuits such as the provision of potions for love. Black Witches were considered to be malicious in their activities. This distinction was removed by Canon Law when it was decided that all supernatural power not emanating from the Church was considered to be demonic.

The very essence of witchcraft in the view of the church is the **demonic pact**. That is, each witch makes a pact with the Devil and renounces Christian baptism. A ceremony would follow where the witch dedicates her immortal soul to the Devil in return for earthbound advantages.

As a result witches have been persecuted throughout Europe since medieval times but in Scotland the phenomenon became extremely intense in the 16th Century. This is probably due to the popular fear of witchcraft after The Reformation, but whatever the cause, it led to the Scottish Witchcraft Act of 1563. This was enacted by Mary Queen of Scots and it led to Scotland being Europe's most aggressive persecutor of witches.

Witch hunts, individual and mass, were commonplace until the start of the 18th century. When the hunt was over and witches were captured they were brought to trial. The trials were held in local church courts; the Courts of Justiciary (High Court usually held in Edinburgh); Circuit Courts; regular local courts (Sheriff and Burgh) and courts set up on an ad hoc basis by the Privy Council.

The evidence used to convict witches would come from their neighbours and other witches. In addition the poor witch would invariably confess guilt after being tortured into doing so by sleep deprivation and by an assortment of physical tortures that are best left to your own imagination.

The most damming evidence however, was the Mark of the Devil. The Devil was believed to mark his disciples after the demonic pact in a parody of Christian Baptism. Witches were examined for blemishes, scars or parts of the body that were insensitive. The insensitive spot would be discovered by pricking with a pin and this was done by professional witch-pickers of which Scotland had a number.

After the witch had been caught, tortured, tried and convicted, all that was left was punishment. This was always execution. The method used was commonly known as 'The Stake'. The victim would be tied to a stake in public view, and then strangled. After this the body was

burned to ash to prevent intervention by the Devil. On a few rare occasions the method was beheading, and even rarer was burning alive.

It should be noted that "consulters of witches are worthy of death in the same manner as practitioners". In other words if you used a witch for whatever reason, and were caught, execution followed. The last execution took place in 1728.

The estimates of the numbers executed between 1563 and 1728 vary between two and four thousand, with the higher number more likely than the lower. There is a small well on the eastern corner of Edinburgh Castle which marks the spot where 300 hundred women accused of witchcraft were executed.

Not all witches were women. Around 15% were men and they were also known as warlocks and this is of interest in terms of the poem.

In 1763 the law was changed, and after this point the courts could only prosecute for pretended witchcraft for which the maximum sentence was one year's imprisonment.

There is no doubt that in the time of Burns witches and the history of witchcraft were widely known, and very probably still feared, by a society governed by church and state. Indeed, members of Burns' family would have been alive at the time of witch hunts.

And so the scene is set for a tale about the Devil and his accessories based on the information gleaned as a young boy in Alloway listening to the stories round the fireside, and those circulating in the village, allied to a common knowledge of witches.

Genesis

Francis Grose, born at Greenford, Middlesex in1731, was the son of an immigrant jeweller from Switzerland. His father was a jeweller in the city of London with a prosperous business who had the distinction of being employed to get up (prepare) the coronation crown of George II. He retired to Richmond, where he was nominated a Justice of the Peace, and died in 1769 leaving his considerable wealth to his children.

Francis was the eldest son and studied as an artist, at which he was quite accomplished. He obtained the office of 'Richmond Herald in the College of Arms' in 1755. In 1763 he relinquished his office in exchange for 600 guineas and joined the Surrey Militia as paymaster and adjutant, rising to the rank of Captain. It appears he was entirely unsuited to such office and as a result, had made serious losses which made a consequent inroad into his own private funds. It was these losses which aroused his energies and stimulated his taste for art once again.

Using the money his father had left him to fund his travels, between 1773 and 1787 he published 6 volumes of the '*Antiquities of England and Wales*' and a '*Classical Dictionary of the Foul Tongue*'. He later produced '*A Provisional Glossary*', '*The Grumbler*' and '*The Olio*'. This work, though produced at great cost, proved successful and profitable and made him determined to illustrate in a similar manner '*The Antiquities of Scotland*'.

Francis was being hosted at Friars Carse by Captain Robert Riddell (1755-1794). Captain Riddell was educated at St Andrews and Edinburgh Universities and joined the Royal Scots as an Ensign. He later enlisted in the Eighty-third Regiment, rising to the rank of Captain in 1771, before retiring in 1783 to Friars Carse, on the Glenriddel Estate, on the banks of the River Nith near to Ellisland. He was a noted antiquarian and was a member of The London Society of Antiquaries.

Friars Carse near Dumfries

Patrick Miller of Dalswinton, the landlord of Robert Burns, is believed to have introduced the poet to Riddell. Burns and Riddell became firm friends and Riddell gave the poet a key to his grounds which contained a decorated cot or hermitage. This led Burns to produce 'Verses in Friars' Carse Hermitage' which was the first of several poems inspired by the friendship. 3

It was Captain Riddell who introduced Francis Grose to Burns in the summer of 1789. The exact date is not known but it would have been either late May or early June. Grose was in Scotland on his travels gathering materials for his book, and during the summer season was residing with Captain Riddell.

Grose's plate of 'Sweetheart Abbey' is marked June 1789 and his plate of 'Lincluden Abbey' is dated August 1789. These plates were etched partially on the spot by a youth who accompanied Grose, whom he called his 'guinea pig'. By the autumn of 1789 he had moved on and was making sketches in Ayrshire.

Burns was immediately struck by Grose enjoying his jolly and archaeological ardour, and grew to like him greatly, and wrote about him the humorous epistle 'On The Late Captain Grose's Peregrinations Thro' Scotland'.

On the 17 July 1789, Burns wrote to Mrs Anna Dunlop of Dunlop saying:

"Captain Grose, the well known Author of the Antiquities of England & Wales, has been through Annandale, Nithsdale & Galloway, in the view of commencing another publication, The Antiquities of Scotland, - As he made his headquarters with Captain Riddell, my nearest neighbour, for these two months, I am intimately acquainted with him: & I have never seen a man of more original observation, anecdote & remark ..... His delight is to steal thro' the country almost unknown, both as favourable to his humour and his business.- I have to the best of my recollection of the old buildings &c. in the County, given him an itinerary thro' Ayr-shire."

Jean Armour Burns described Grose as one of the funniest, laughing,

fat, good-natured men she ever saw. When he called at Ellisland he took a glass of rum and water; never dined; *'for they were always gaun to Captain Riddel's for their dinner.'* Jean also recalls Burns writing to her father (James Armour) to draw some antiquities about the West Country but she was not present when the bargain was made about Alloway Kirk. 4

Burns asked Grose to include Alloway Kirk in his book principally as his father's remains were interred there. Grose apparently agreed, provided Burns would write a ghost story to accompany the sketch in the publication.

According to Gilbert Burns it happened as follows:

'When my father feued his little property near Alloway Kirk, the wall of the churchyard had gone to ruin, and cattle had free liberty to pasture in it. My father and two or three neighbours joined in an application to the town-council of Ayr, who were superiors of the adjoining land, for liberty to rebuild it, and raised by subscription a sum for enclosing this ancient cemetery with a wall: hence he came to consider it as his burial-place, and we learned that reverence for it people generally have for the burial-place of their ancestors. My brother was living in Ellisland , when Captain Grose, on his peregrinations through Scotland, stayed some time at Carse House in the neighbourhood, with Captain Robert Riddel of Glenriddel, a particular friend of my brother's. The antiquary and the poet were 'unco pack and thick thegither'. Robert requested Captain Grose, when he should come to Ayrshire, that he would make a drawing of Alloway Kirk, as it was the burial-place of his father, where he himself had a sort of claim to lay down his bones when they should no longer be serviceable to him; and added, by way of encouragement, that it was the scene of many a good story of witches and apparitions, of which he knew the captain was fond. The captain agreed to the request, provided that the poet would furnish a witch-story, to be printed along with it. "Tam o' Shanter" was produced on this occasion, and was first published in Grose's Antiqities of Scotland'

The deal thus cemented during the summer of 1789 led to Burns producing the poem some 18 months later.

In June of 1790, Burns wrote to Captain Grose providing him with the information on stories he (Burns) had heard. The letter contained the following:

'Among the many Witch Stories I have heard relating to Alloway Kirk, I distinctly remember only two or three.

Upon a stormy night, amid whirling squalls of wind and bitter blasts of hail, in short, on such a night as the devil would chuse to take the air in, a farmer or farmer's servant was plodding and plashing homeward with his plough-irons on his shoulder, having been getting repairs on them at the neighbouring smithy. His way lay by the Kirk of Alloway, and being rather on the anxious lookout, in approaching a place so well known to be a favourite haunt of the devil and the devil's friends and emissaries, he was struck aghast by discovering through the horrors of the storm and the stormy night, a light, which on his nearer approach, plainly shewed itself to be from the haunted edifice. Whether he had been fortified from above on his devout supplication, as is customary with people when they suspect the immediate presence of Satan; or whether, according to another custom, he had got courageously drunk at the smithy, I will not pretend to determine; but so it was that he ventured to go up to, nay into the very kirk. As good luck would have it, his temerity came off unpunished. The members of the infernal junto were all out on some midnight business or other, and he saw nothing but a kind of kettle or caldron, depending from the roof, over the fire simmering some heads of unchristened children, limbs of executed malefactors &c. for the business of the night. It was, in for a penny, in for a pound, with the honest ploughman: so without ceremony he unhooked the caldron from off the fire, and pouring out the damnable ingredients, inverted it on his head, and carried it fairly home, where it remained long in the family a living evidence of truth of the story.

Another story which I can prove to be equally authentic was as follows.

the story of a tale

On a market day in the town of Ayr, a farmer from Carrick, and consequently whose way lay by the very gate of Alloway kirk-yard, in order to cross the river Doon at the old bridge, which is about two or three hundred yards further on than the said gate, had been detained by his business, 'till by the time he reached Alloway, it was the wizard hour, between night and morning. Though he was terrified, with the blaze streaming from the kirk, yet as it is a well-known fact that to turn back on these occasions is running by far the greater risk of mischief, he prudently advanced on his road. When he reached the gate of the kirk-yard, he was surprised and entertained, through the ribs and arches of an old gothic window which still faces the highway, to see a dance of witches merrily footing it round their old sooty blackguard master, who was keeping them alive with the powers of his bag-pipe. The farmer stopping his horse to observe them a little, could plainly descry the faces of many old women of his acquaintance in the neighbourhood. How the gentleman was dressed tradition does not say; but the ladies were all in their smocks: and one of them happening unluckily to have a smock which was considerably too short to answer all the purpose of that piece of dress, our farmer was so tickled that he involuntary burst out with a loud laugh, "Well luppen Maggy wi' the short sark!" and recollecting himself, instantly spurred his horse to the top of his speed. I need not mention the universally known fact, that no diabolical power can pursue you beyond the middle of a running stream. Luckily it was for the poor farmer that the river Doon was so near, for notwithstanding the speed of his horse, which was a good one, against he reached the middle of the arch of the bridge, and consequently the middle of the stream, the pursuing, vengeful, hags, were so close at his heels, that one of them actually sprung to seize him; but it was too late nothing was on her side of the stream but the horses tail, which immediately gave way to her infernal grip, as if blasted by a stroke of lightning: but the farmer was beyond her reach. However, the unsightly, tailless condition of the vigorous steed was to the last hour of the noble creature's life, an awful warning to the Carrick farmers, not to stay too late in Ayr markets.

The last relation I shall give, though equally true, is not so well identified as the two former, with regard to the scene: but as the best authorities give it for Alloway, I shall relate it.

On a summer's evening, about that time that Nature puts on her sables to mourn the expiry of the cheerful day, a shepherd boy belonging to a farmer in the immediate neighbourhood of Alloway Kirk, had just folded his charge, and was returning home. As he passed the kirk, in the adjoining field, he fell in with a crew of men and women, who were busy pulling stems of the plant ragwort. He observed that as each person pulled a ragwort, he or she got astride of it and called out, "Up horsie!" on which the ragwort flew off, like Pegasus, through the air with its rider. The foolish boy likewise pulled his ragwort, and cried with the rest "Up horsie!" and, strange to tell, he flew away with the company. The first stage at which the cavalcade stopt, was a merchants wine cellar in Bordeaux, where, without a by your leave, they quaffed away at the best the cellar could afford, until the morning, foe to the imps and works of darkness, threatened to throw light on the matter, and frightened them from their carousals.

The poor shepherd lad, being equally a stranger to the scene and the liquor, heedlessly got himself drunk and when the rest took horse, he fell asleep, and was found the next day by some of the people belonging to the merchant. Somebody that understood Scotch, asking him what he was, he said he was such-a-one's herd in Alloway; and by some means or other getting home again, he lived to tell the world the wondrous tale.

I am &c. &c.
Rob Burns'

The ragwort story had been used before by Burns in the poem 'Address to the Deil', where he writes:

Let warlocks grim, an' wither'd hags,
Tell how wi' you, on ragweed nags,
They skim the muirs an' dizzy crags,

Wi' wicked speed;
And in kirk-yards renew their leagues,
Owre howkit dead.

Burns combined the first two stories to create the poem changing some of the details and adding even more to it. He also uses the ending of the second story as the final moral of Tam o' Shanter.

What the three stories do show is that Burns had a great deal of knowledge regarding the activities and rituals of witches and their relationship to Satan.

The letters of Burns sent to Captain Grose give the accepted version of where the story of Tam o' Shanter originated, but there is another possibility in an account coming from Kirkcudbrightshire in 1750, nine years before Robert Burns was born and forty years before Tam o' Shanter was written.

St John's Town of Dalry is situated on a hillside close to the banks of the River Ken in an area generally known as the Glenkens. The village is now quite large, being an ideal place to locate to tour the Southern Upland Way, but it was formerly known as Auld Clachan.

Around the middle of the 18th century the village stretched up the hill with a spattering of low cottages, some weaver's homes and a few businesses and hostelries. It is from this time that a story arises of witches and a chase, where one witness to the event, claims to have seen a black, smudged mark, shaped like a woman's hand on the rump of a mare. As Tam o' Shanter would have it, now to our tale.

Adam Forrester was the laird of Knocksheen, situated about 5 miles by road from Dalry on route to Drumbuie. The name Knocksheen is taken from the Gaelic ncoc sidhean which means "hill of the fairies", so Adam was no stranger to the supernatural. Knocksheen farmhouse still exists today and can be found at map reference NX 577 825.

Adam enjoyed a dram or two and his favourite haunt was an inn that stood up the hill in the centre of the village (now the street is known as Midtown in modern Dalry) and operated by a buxom widow with the surname of Hare, who had been christened 'Lucky' by her customers. The inn was not large but comfortable with peat fires to warm the clientele, good company and enough drink to ease the mood. On a cold winter night with a blustering wind Adam Forrester sat in the inn toasting his toes at the fire, drinking with his friends and forgetting the time. It was around midnight that Adam decided to head for his home, left his friends shouting farewell and, jamming his dark blue bonnet on his head, took his mare's bridle from the iron ring in the wall of the inn. He mounted the beast and clattered down the hill toward the ford over the River Ken near to the old church.

Dalry Parish Church is in the same spot today on an incline above the Kirkyard and dates from 1832. Next to the current church is the Gordon Aisle which is part of the original church built in 1546.

As he reached the church the horse stopped dead in her tracks, neighed and shook her head alerting Adam to what was a startling sight. The old kirk was ablaze with a light so bright it could not have been lit by human hands and from inside a noise reached his ears. It was not the usual sound of holy psalmody but screeching, skirling and profanities that were truly shocking. Rising above the din Adam could recognise the voice of the woman who had only just before afforded him the hospitality of her inn, 'Lucky' Hare.

Adam dismounted and hitched his mare to a tree and made his way, probably unsteadily, stumbling over tombstones to the window of the church nearest him and standing on tip toe he could see inside. A vision of iniquity met his gaze. Whirling and cavorting in unholy glee was a band of crones, including one 'Lucky' Hare, that Adam recognised as local worthies. Righteous indignation overcame prudence and Adam banged on the window with his whip and roared out "Ho there, Lucky my lass, ye'll no deny this the morn."

The effect was immediate and by some magic sleight the light went out and the revelry turned to raucous rage. The hags streamed out of the church to take their revenge and it seemed to Adam they were airborne.

Dalry Parish Church

The Witches Score (photograph courtesy of Keith Kirk)

Adam, however, had a good start and reached his mare. As he mounted the horse reared and took off at full speed down the steep slope to the ford across the River Ken. Splashing across the water the mare continued on up Waterside Hill racing for safety and home.

Unable to cross a running stream the covey of hags led by 'Lucky' Hare flew off three miles downstream to the Bridge of Ken to cross over. On broomsticks flying faster than the wind they caught up with Adam on the hill and clutching the poor mare's tail they stripped it of every hair. As 'Lucky' stretched out and slapped the rump of the horse Adam flung himself to the ground calling to God for help. In his desperate strait he recalled long discarded lore and drew a rough circle on the hillside all around him and his mare with his sword.

At the holy name and circle the snarls and screams of the hags turned to frustration and they dispersed as dawn broke. Adam was so thankful to have survived the encounter; the dread of his reception

from his wife on so late a return home was quite negated. When he came to unsaddle the poor horse, he saw the black smudged mark of Lucky's hand on the mare's grey rump. It remained there, impervious to all attempts to remove it, and was evidence for his doubting spouse of the strange tale he had related. As further proof for all to see, there appeared overnight a strange smutty circle on Waterside Hill, and there it has remained.

The circle is located on what is now known as 'The Score' and is situated at map reference NX 604 818. It was kept clear for many years by the Forrester family, but is now overgrown; it can still be distinguished nevertheless.

It is suspected that Burns found out about the above story from Dr Robert Trotter who was a native of the area, although there is no documented evidence of this in either the letters or works of Burns.

Dr Robert Trotter (1735 - 1815) was a surgeon at New Galloway for over thirty years and he wrote several poetical works. He was celebrated in his day for discovering, in 1776, the cure for a disease called yaws which is a particularly loathsome infection of the skin, bones and joints, and was once the scourge of Europe.

It is widely reported that he was acquainted with Burns and was a guide for Burns and John Syme during Burns' tour of Galloway. During the tour Burns stayed with the Gordon family at Kenmure, for whom Trotter was the family physician. The family had a dog, Echo, which was unwell, and Trotter refused to treat the animal resulting in his dismissal from the Gordon family's service. The dog died and the family prevailed upon Burns to write something which resulted in 'Epitaph on a Lapdog'.

A similar version of this tale, originating in Galloway, is given by Cunningham which states that the farmer cut himself free with his sword. On reaching his home the farmer found a woman's hand in his horse's tail. The next day a neighbour's wife is discovered with a bloody hand. She was accused of witchcraft and burned. 5

The main issue relating to this tale pre-dating Tam o' Shanter is that the new bridge over the River Ken, about three miles south of Dalry, was built in 1796 by public and private subscription. It was destroyed by flood in 1811 and rebuilt during 1820-21 by John Rennie.

If the description of the tale is accurate, in so far as the witches crossed the Brig O' Ken to catch Adam, then they must have done so after 1796 as before this date the crossing was by ferry or fording the river. There is another bridge across the Ken Water, just to the north of Dalry which existed in the mid 18th century, and it may be that to the south of the village there was an older wooden bridge. Perhaps the tale has been adjusted in the telling, as often happens with stories passed by word of mouth. Whether the story of Adam Forrester is an inspiration or imitation of Tam o' Shanter is a decision only the reader can make, but it is a cracking good tale and adds to the flavour of a beautiful part of the world.

Whatever the origin, the poem Tam o' Shanter was written by Robert Burns based on local stories and folk tales as others have done before him. Homer wrote his great poem the *Iliad* based on memories, folk tales, traditions, myths and genealogies. Some of his descriptions have proven to be uncannily accurate according to subsequent archaeology, leading to the poem by Homer being the accepted version of events that happened over three millennia ago.

Tam o' Shanter was printed by Grose as a sequel to his description of Alloway Kirk, being prefaced by the following remarks;

'The church is also famous for being the place wherein the witches and warlocks used to hold their infernal meetings on Sabbaths, and prepare for their magical unctions. Here, too, they used to amuse themselves with dancing to the pipes of the muckle horned deil. Divers stories of these horrid rites are still current, one of which my worthy friend Mr Burns has here favoured me with in verse.'

'The Antiquities of Scotland' was finished in 1791, and consisted of two volumes with 190 views and a letterpress.

Prior to the work being published Captain Grose headed to Ireland where he intended to continue his work with a volume on that country.

In May 1791 he reached Dublin where he resided with a Mr Hone. It was here that he was seized by an epileptic fit of which he died on 12 May 1791. He was buried in Drumcondra Churchyard near Dublin.

During his time in Edinburgh he came to the attention of John Kay, the miniature painter and caricaturist, who represented him in his 'Edinburgh Portraits' in the act of deciphering an inscription on an ancient ruin. It is this portrait that is reproduced in many publications of the works of Robert Burns.

Setting

The poem is set in South Ayrshire and starts in the town of Ayr and takes us on a journey to Shanter farm via the haunted old church in Alloway and the Brig O' Doon.

Burns was very familiar with Ayr and was obviously impressed by the town and its residents, as he indicates in lines 15 and 16 of the poem;

(Auld Ayr wham ne'er a town surpasses,
For honest men and bonny lasses.)

The Ayr of Burns' day was much different to the town we know today and the geography and topography of the town is crucial to any understanding of the poem.

The Royal Burgh of Ayr was established between 1203 and 1206, and was set on the south side of the River Ayr. The main part of the town set around what is now known as the High Street. Until the completion of the New Brig in 1789, the only crossing of the river Ayr was the Auld Brig.

The Ayr of the 1770's had hardly increased in size since medieval times and was a community of merchants, tradesmen, fishermen, sailors and the residence of a number of other individuals of independent fortune. The town layout was based on the converging High Street and Sandgate. The meeting of these two streets was known then, as it is today, as Market Cross.

Further up High Street was (and is) Fish Cross which hosted the Meal Market. In the middle of the Sandgate the 'Town Gaol' could be found. Off the High Street near the river sat the Auld Kirk of Ayr, just as it does today having been moved there in 1654.

The town had two schools, the English School and the Burgh School both of which were to the west of the Sandgate. Further west were the remains of the Citadel which had been erected during the Cromwellian occupation. The harbour sat further west still, with piers on both banks of the river.

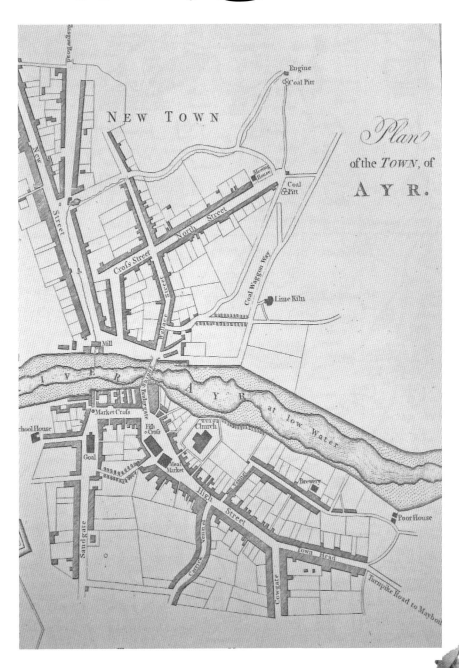

Across the Auld Brig was the 'New Town', known better today as Newton upon Ayr. The New Town burgh was in St Quivox parish and also formed the community of Wallacetown. Wallacetown was established by Sir Thomas Wallace of Craigie, who laid out Wallace Street. About 1760 his descendent, also Sir Thomas Wallace and father of Anna Dunlop of Dunlop (the famous correspondent of Burns), began to fue out houses and gardens, thus expanding the population of the area.

The Royal Burgh had a population of around 3,000, with the New Town adding around another 1,000. There were nine incorporated trades including weavers, dyers, tailors, shoemakers, coopers and fleshers. The principal manufacturing consisted of soap, leather and weaving. The port had over 30 vessels involved in foreign trade, coastal trade and fishing. There were 36 retail shops including grocery, hardware, haberdashery and broad cloth. Between the river and the top of High Street as many as 24 public houses or Inns existed in the Royal Burgh alone.

The town had 2 market days each week, on Tuesday and Friday, and also had four annual fairs.

Ayr was a bustling, busy county town, with market days and fairs drawing many people into town from the country, and one can well imagine the scenes that Burns sets at the start of his poem of traders and locals heading home or into the ale house.

On leaving Ayr to head for home, Tam and Meg wend their way through the storm to the place where the most colourful part of the tale takes place, Alloway's Auld Kirk.

Alloway Auld Kirk was allegedly built in 1516 and served as a parish church until 1691 when Alloway was joined to the parish of Ayr. On the south wall of the kirk, above the window, there is a stone giving the date 1516. Closer inspection of the upper lintel of the window shows a stone with a sword carved into it. This appears even older than the stones surrounding it and may have been recovered from a grave and used in the construction of the building.

Alloway Auld Kirk

The Kirk fell into disrepair during the following 50 years or so but was re-roofed in 1740 and, until 1752, the building was used as a school then it again fell vacant. The roof collapsed again when Robert was a boy.

When the sketch was done By Captain Grose, he shows some roof timbers in place but this may not be entirely accurate. In 1786 the Council granted a sum of £15 to put a new roof on the building and convert it into a meeting place or a school. The sketch by Grose was in 1789 and either the work had not been completed or he altered it to suit his own purpose.

Despite an effort by William Burnes and some villagers to repair the neglect to the kirk yard, the church itself was ruinous and deserted and was no doubt a catalyst for the fertile imagination of a young Burns already influenced by stories from Betty Davidson.

As it stands today the kirk has an internal wall built between the north and south walls, dividing the kirk into two separate spaces. This wall is an addition and would not have been there when Burns was familiar with the building.

On entering the kirk yard, the first sight is of the grave of William Burns, with his name spelt in that way, despite the fact he never altered from the original Burnes.

The church bell is still in place above the east gable and is easily seen on ascending the steps into the kirk yard. The bell was a source of local controversy in 1789 when the magistrates of Ayr attempted to remove it and the local people "repelled the attempt by open force".

Moving to the left around to the south side of the church, there is a door which has the date above it, which allows a view of the inside through some iron railings. Placed in this room are two mort safes used to protect the graves. Grave robbing has been around for over 2000 years but between the 16th and 18th centuries, medical research gave a boost to the trade in Scotland. Burke and Hare were not the only ones to make a living in such a manner and a mort safe was set to prevent the body being exhumed.

Mort Safes Alloway Kirk

Saining Bowl

Brig O' Doon

There is also a saining bowl built into the wall of the kirk. This derives from the archaic Scots word 'sain' which means to make the sign of the cross. A saining bowl was an outside font where pilgrims or others not allowed inside, such as lepers, could use the holy water to bless themselves.

The graveyard holds many interesting graves, including one of the 13 children of Francis Anna Dunlop, the patron of Robert Burns.

Just across the road from the Kirk, about a hundred or so yards further on, is the Brig O' Doon, dating from the beginning of the 15th century, which in the 18th century was the main crossing of the river by bridge between Kyle and Carrick.

The bridge would have been a busy thoroughfare for farmers and others travelling to Ayr on market and fair days. It would also have been used to transport stone from the nearby quarry, and the goods from Alloway Mill, which was further downriver towards the sea.

After the chase Tam then makes his way home to Shanter Farm, which depending on the publication you read, appears to have well into double figures for different locations of the farm. This confusion probably arises as the farm no longer exists.

In the 1827 publication 'A Picture of Scotland Volume 1' by Robert Chambers, it is related that the farm house and outbuildings were annexed and that a new cottage was built using the materials. Chambers describes the farm as being about a mile from Turnberry on a rise, in the direction of Kirkoswald, and within site of the castle ruins. However, he also relates that the occupant of the farm during the life of Burns was one Thomas Reid, who wore a distinctive blue bonnet and rode a grey horse about the countryside, he asserts that it was on this individual that Burns based his Tam o' Shanter. Given this assertion it may well be that his placement of the farm is askew but nevertheless it does prove that the farm itself was demolished prior to 1827.

A map drawn in 1694 clearly sites Shanter farm close to what is now the village of Maidens. In the 18th century the village did not exist as

it now is and the name stems from two prominent rocks known locally as the Maidens.

The farm was located quite near the present day Shanter Riding School and Farm. It sat on the east side of what is now the A719 road, about half a mile south-east of Maidens village, on a mound or mote to the east side of the disused Ayr to Girvan railway line. The site of the farm can be found at map reference NS 218074. 6

The name Shanter comes from the Gaelic 'sean tor' meaning old mound. The photograph shows the area as it is now and the farm would have been located near the slight rise in the centre.

The site of Shanter Farm

The Route

The route used by Tam on that fateful night obviously starts in Ayr but where exactly is not known. What is certain is that it was not at what is now the Tam o' Shanter Inn in High Street, Ayr. In the mid 18th century, this building was the dwelling house of the Shearer family.

In 1748, Elizabeth Wilson sold the property to James Shearer for nine pounds ten shillings sterling. The price was low, even for those days, suggesting the house may have been run down. By April 1753 the house had been enlarged to make one large tenement of two stories covering the whole width of the plot. The southmost part projected on to the street and had three rooms upstairs and a small apartment and shop downstairs. The rest of the building was the family home of James and Annie Shearer. It would remain a family home for another 90 years and it would be more than a century before it became famous as the Tam o' Shanter Inn. 7

The reason Tam was in Ayr on a market day is not known. It may be he was in town to buy or sell goods, but from the poem it seems he was travelling home without a great deal of baggage, if any.

The tale puts him in an ale house, enjoying the company and the ale, and this could be done quite easily in Ayr at the time. There were over twenty pubs or ale houses between the harbour and the top of the high street and an unknown number of shebeens (drinking dens) where the locals concocted and sold their own brew.

It is probable that Tam was at a market that day either at the Market Cross or Fish Cross and would have gravitated to somewhere around the centre of the High Street.

'A New Map of Ayrshire Comprehending Kyle, Cunningham and Carrick' was published in 1775 by Andrew and Moysten Armstrong in 6 sheets. There are reservations as regards total accuracy of these maps, but they nevertheless provide a good view of the county at that time.

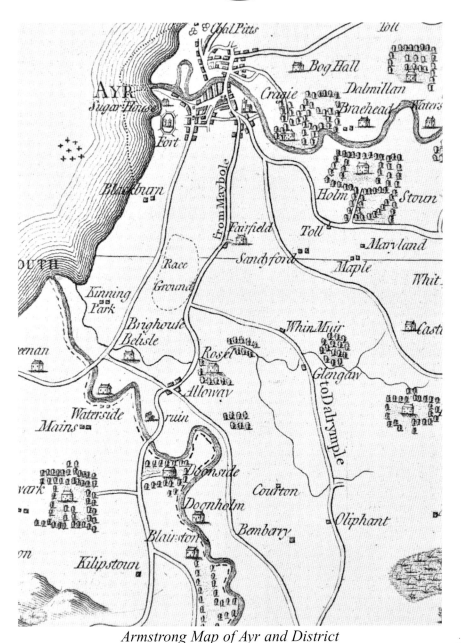

Armstrong Map of Ayr and District

The Ayrshire Turnpike Acts of 1767 and 1774 meant that Ayrshire was being covered with additional new roads to meet the demand of the increasing passenger and goods traffic. The roads of the early part of the century were so poor that wheeled traffic was impossible, but by the time of Tam's great ride the situation was different with many Turnpikes (toll roads) and other thoroughfares. There was a road from Ayr to Maybole which continued to Dailly and Girvan and all the other villages of Carrick in this vicinity. This road ran on the east side of the race ground (old race course), through Alloway village and crossed the river Doon by means of The Brig O' Doon. Another smaller road ran parallel nearer the coast and through Belleisle estate.

The Ayrshire road system has been almost completely changed since the Armstrong map and of the roads leading south from Ayr, only the Dalmellington road and the road from Sandgate to the Low Bridge of Doon remain relatively unchanged. The big new estates (18th century) of Belleisle and Rozelle have enclosed parts of the old roads.

So, should he have chosen to, Tam could have ridden along using the road networks of the day but the poem tells us he decided on a short cut or detour;

Tam skelpit on thro' dub and mire,
Despising wind and rain and fire. (lines 81-82)

This would suggest that Tam left Ayr via the Foul Vennel (Carrick Street) or the Cow Vennel (Alloway Street) and travelled south through the Burrowfield. This was an area of sand-dunes, wastes of grass and whins and would have led him nearer to the coastal road indicated on the Armstrong map. The Burrowfield began along a line from the Townhead by Dalblair Road and Fullerton Street to the sea.

The Burrowfield included, to the east, the Burrow Muir and nearer the sea the Town Common. This was a desolate area up until late in the 18th century. There were only three streams above ground in the path of Tam, the Black Burn, the Sergeants Burn and the Curtecan also known as the Slaphouse Burn. Tam's route lay across the Common to the Curtecan, as the other two were not of any size and would not have

the story of a tale

needed a ford or bridge to cross, and thereafter through the Barony of Alloway.

Tam's progress is given as follows;

By this time he was cross the ford,
Where in the snaw the chapman smoor'd;
And past the birks and meikle stane,
Where drunken Charlie brak's necks-bane;
And thro' the whins and by the cairn
Where hunters fand the murder'd bairn;
And near the thorn, aboon the well,
Where Mungo's mither hang'd hersel'. (Lines 89-96)

This is the most descriptive part of the journey and was a well known area to Burns who grew up close by. It can still be walked today, with the understanding that the exact features have changed a little and the fact that the Burns used some poetic licence when creating his narrative.

John Skilling, resident of Alloway, member of Alloway Burns Club and a Past President of The Robert Burns World Federation, has a great deal of knowledge regarding Burns in Alloway and this route. He frequently gives of his own time to take parties and individuals (including the author) a walk along the above 8 lines. This is something not to be missed if you have the good fortune to persuade him out on a dreich day.

However, even without a guide, it is a walk worth undertaking and the easiest way to do it is to travel along the B7024 from Ayr (Monument Road) and park at Rozelle House. This will also give you the opportunity to view some of the Goudie paintings which hang there.

On leaving the estate on foot turn right and walk back toward Ayr. Across the road is Belleisle Golf Course and a few hundred yards further down you will see Longlands Park on your right. Just opposite there you can enter the golf course through the wooden fencing. Continue on until you are clear of the trees and turn left toward the 15th Tee.

If you turn around you can see the Slaphouse Cottage jutting into the course.

Slaphouse Cottage

Directly in front of you can also seen a stockbridge. You have to be careful around this area, particularly in summer as it is a busy public golf course.

This stockbridge crosses the Slaphouse Burn. This is the water where the chapman smothered in the snow at the ford. However, there is no indication of a ford anywhere in the area. The bridge formed part of the old road and Ayr Town Council minutes of 7 June 1756 indicate a payment to John Donald, an Ayr mason, for the building of a bridge over the Slaphouse Burn near to the Slaphouse. On June 29th 1757 it is noted that John McClure, the late tenant of Slaphouse, is claiming that to build the bridge the Magistrates and Council of Ayr made a road through his grass and corn in the summer of 1755, in order that materials may be led to the site. He wanted thirty pounds Scots (fifteen shillings sterling) in compensation and was paid twenty. 8

This makes it clear that on the line of the old road there was a bridge across the burn four years before Burns was born. It may well be that the bridge was built on the site of an old ford across the burn, and the drowning preceded the birth of Burns and was related to him by a relative, although there is no evidence to confirm this.

Another reason for having a ford could be poetic. Burns would not want to have a bridge featuring twice in the narrative. The crescendo of the poem is the Brig O' Doon and he could have written the lines to ensure this had the effect of heightening the chase. In 'Address to the Deil', he has the Devil use water kelpies to haunt a ford to lure travellers to their destruction. The type of misfortune befalling the poor chapman is not very far estranged from this concept.

Whatever the reason, the Slaphouse or Curtecan is where Tam crossed toward the birks an' meikle stane.

When you continue across the stockbridge you are now following in the tracks of Meg.

Stockbridge

The stone placed where Charlie came to grief

According to local tradition, the meikle stane was about 90 yards south of the Monument Road entrance to Belleisle. As you walk on, keep into the side with the woods on your left until you cross the path to Belleisle. About 135 yards from this pathway, on the left just off the fairway, you will see a stone which lies roughly where *'Charlie brak's neck bane'*. Where the original *'meikle stane'* went is unknown but any large obstacle would have been removed during the construction of the golf course.

If you now enter the wood, a short way in you will find a path and should continue along it toward Alloway. Carry on until you emerge onto the road (B7024) about 200 yards short of the village. Continue on past Burns Cottage (you can always return), and turn right into Greenfield Avenue. Then take the first left into Baird Road and the first right into Cairn Crescent following the road round.

When the book 'Ayrshire in the Time of Burns' was published in 1959, the cairn *'where hunters found the murder'd bairn'* was still in existence. It was marked by an ash tree and surrounded by a light iron railing. It would have been some distance to the right of the road Tam was on.

Due to the development of the area for housing in 1963 the cairn was lost. Using stones from the original cairn a monument was built close to the original site in Cairn Crescent which you will see as you walk along. It is four feet high and is mounted with a bronze plaque reading "'And Through the whins and by the cairn' to perpetuate that eventful journey of Tam to Alloway Kirk. This cairn was re-erected through the co-operation of Ayr Town Council, the Burns Federation and John Dickie and Son Ltd, builders. July 1965."

Two seats flank the cairn where the weary can rest for a moment and these were presented by The Scottish Society of Burns Clubs of Australia and the Tam o' Shanter Burns Club, Ndola, Zambia.

Continue on around the Crescent and then turn right (Baird Road) and right again (Cambusdoon Drive) back onto the road (B7024). Kirk Alloway is not too far along on your right hand side, and of course

you should visit it. Before you do, there is still the ride of Meg to follow to Mungo's Well, which is about 100 yards west of the Kirk.

The road runs over a disused railway tunnel near the Kirk and you must go through this tunnel. To get there, cross the road into Murdoch's Lone and take the left hand footpath. Walking away from the Auld Kirk on your left, you will see a pathway down to the old railway which is now itself a path. Go down to this path, turning left walking along toward the tunnel. Go through the tunnel under the road and as you emerge on your right you will see the sign placed by Alloway Burns Club in 2008 indicating the site of the well.

St Mungo is the Patron saint of Glasgow and Alloway Auld Kirk is thought to have been dedicated to him as Glasgow Cathedral owned land locally at Carcluie.

There is no direct evidence that the Mungo whose mother hanged herself is indeed St Mungo but that is widely considered to be the case and accepted as a fiction. 9

St Mungo lived at the turn of the 6th and 7th century but the only surviving information about him comes from the 12th century, making it difficult to determine what is fact and what is fiction. His mother was Tenew (later St Tenew), daughter of King Llew or Loth, after whom Lothian is named.

Tenew allegedly had an affair with her cousin Owain, resulting in the birth of Mungo. As sex outwith marriage was a crime punishable by death, when her father discovered she was pregnant he was obliged to follow the law of the times. She was thrown from Trapain Law, a large hill near Edinburgh, but survived the fall. Consequently she was cast adrift in a coracle as Loth was of the opinion she may be a witch. She drifted to the coast of Fife landing at Culross where St Serf ran a religious settlement. She was rescued and had the child, who was named Kentigern. The child was promptly given the nickname Mungo by St Serf.

The Cairn

Mungo's Well

Nowhere in these histories does Tenew commit suicide, and certainly not in Alloway as she lived some considerable distance away. We are left with the notion that either it is a work of fiction by Burns or it is some other hapless soul who lived in the area and also had a son named Mungo.

After seeing the well, you should retrace your steps to Murdoch's Lone and walk back to the road and into the Auld Kirk yard. If you go to your left, to the south side of the Kirk, the side Tam would have approached, you will see a small window through which a man on horseback could view the 'winnock bunker in the east' and all the evening's festivities.

South window Alloway Auld Kirk

When you leave cross the road and turn right past the front of Alloway Parish Church and, just before you reach the Brig O' Doon Hotel, turn left and follow the road down to the bridge.

You will now be at the place where poor Meg was mutilated by the witch and you can stand on the very spot. The rest of Tam's journey must have been an anticlimax all the way to the farm, where Kate would be waiting nursing her wrath.

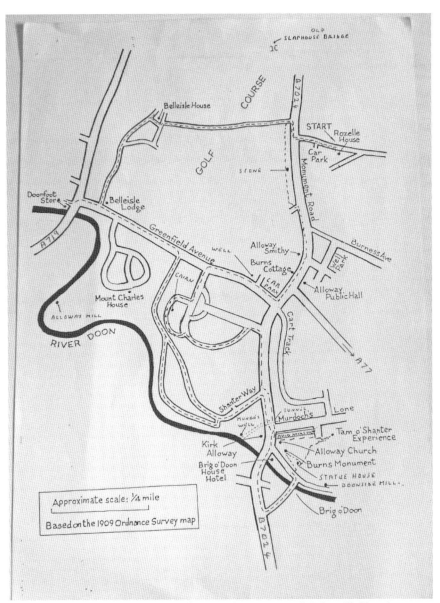

Map of the route in Alloway (courtesy of John Skilling)

Background on the Characters

In the summer of 1775, William Burnes was struggling at Mount Oliphant, but he decided to send Robert away to continue his schooling and Robert recalls the circumstances in a letter to Dr John Moore dated 2 August 1787.

Dr Moore was born at Stirling in 1729 and qualified in medicine at Glasgow University. After service as a Surgeons Mate in the Duke of Argyle's Regiment, he continued his studies in Paris. He was a companion and tutor of nobility and published on the society and manners of several European nations. In the autumn of 1786, Mrs Frances Anna Dunlop sent him a copy of the Kilmarnock Edition. Moore was intrigued by the work and replied to Mrs Dunlop, asking her to tell Robert to get in touch with him.

Burns delayed writing to Moore through some fear of inadequacy as he relates to Mrs Dunlop by letter from Edinburgh on 15 January 1787;

'I wished to have written to Dr Moore before I wrote to you; but though, every day since I received yours of Dec. 30, the idea, the wish to write to him, has constantly pressed on my thoughts, yet I could not for my soul set about it. I know his fame and character, and I am one of the "sons of little men." To write him a mere matter-of-fact affair, like a merchants order, would be disgracing the little character I have: and to write to the author of the View of Society and Manners, a letter of sentiment – I declare every artery runs cold at the thought. I shall try, however, to write to him tomorrow or the next day. His kind interposition on my behalf I have already experienced, as a gentleman waited on me the other day, on the part of Lord Eglinton, with ten guineas, by way of subscription for two copies of my next edition.'

It is clear from this letter that Burns was aware of Moore's accomplishments and had an inflated notion of Moore's literary standing. Burns would almost certainly have been disposed to impress the great man. As a consequence, it may be that the letter of August

1787, now commonly known as the autobiographical letter, whilst accurate, was written by the poet to maximise his talents and impress where possible.

In this letter to Moore Burns writes;

'Another circumstance in my life which made very considerable alterations in my mind and manners was, I spent my seventeenth summer [1775] on a smuggling coast a good distance from home at a noted school, to learn Mensuration, Surveying, Dialling, &c. in which I made pretty good progress.- But I made greater progress in the knowledge of mankind.- The contraband trade was at the time very successful; scenes of swaggering riot and roaring dissipation were as yet new to me; and I was no enemy of social life.- Here, though I learned to look unconcernedly on a large tavern bill, and mix without fear in a drunken squabble, yet I went on with a high hand in my Geometry; till the sun entered Virgo, a month which is always a carnival in my bosom, a charming Fillette who lived next door to the school overset my Trigonometry and set me off in a tangent from the sphere of my studies.- I struggled on with my Sines and my Co-sines for a few days more; but stepping out to the garden one charming noon, to take the sun's altitude, I met my Angel,

"Like Prosperine gathering flowers,
Herself a fairer flower" –

It was vain to think of doing any more good at school.- The remaining week I staid, I did nothing but craze the faculties of my soul about her, or steal out to meet with her; and the two last nights of my stay in the country, had sleep been a mortal sin, I was innocent.'

The Fillette was Peggy Thomson, for whom was written '*A Song Composed in August*' and the quote on Prosperine comes from Milton's Paradise Lost, a work that was a firm favourite of Burns and was to lend inspiration to Tam o' Shanter.

This was Robert Burns' first real stay away from home, and it must have been an eye opener for a sixteen year old of his background and upbringing. Smuggling was endemic on the Ayrshire coast, with brandy and tea the foremost contraband. It does not need a great deal of imagination to conjure a mental image of what was going on in these small coastal towns and villages awash with smuggled alcohol.

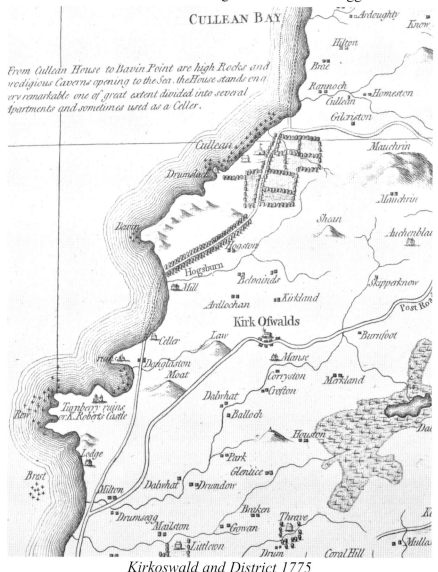

Kirkoswald and District 1775

In the *Annals of the Parish 1761* John Galt writes:

'It was in this year that the great smuggling trade corrupted all the west coast, especially the laigh lands about the Troon and the Loans. The tea was going like chaff, the brandy like well-water, and the wastry of all things was terrible. There was nothing minded but the riding of cadgers by day, and the excisemen by night – and battles between the smugglers and the king's men, both by sea and land. There was a continual drunkenness and debauchery; and our session, that was but the lip of this whirlpool of iniquity, had an awful time o't. I did all that was within the power of nature to keep my people from the contagion: I preached sixteen times from the text, "Render unto Caeser the things that are Caeser's." I visited, and I exhorted; I warned and I prophesised; I told them that, although the money came in like sclate stones, it would go like the snow off the dyke. But for all I could do, the evil got in among us, and we had no less than three contested bastard bairns upon our hands at one time, which was a thing never heard of in a parish of the shire of Ayr since the Reformation.' 10

Whilst this relates to Troon and district, it was a similar picture up and down the county. With the smuggling came profits which were a blessing to the poor along the coast, and no amount of preaching at them would be a deterrent.

There is no doubt that Kirkoswald was a pretty tough place to be in 1775. The parish has a deeply indented coastline extending for six miles along the Carrick shore, with many bays and coves and was very different to the Ayr and Dalrymple that Burns knew. It provided a perfect terrain for those engaged in contraband running. By 1790, this smuggling was accepted in large part, as evinced by the parish minister Reverend Mathew Biggar who wrote;

'Though the character and behaviour of those engaged in this business were, for the most part, in other respects good; yet, without doubt, it produced very bad effects on the industry of the people, and gave them a taste for luxury and finery that spoiled the simplicity of manners which formerly prevailed in this parish.'

It was a favourite destination for the smuggling vessels from the Isle of Man which brought French lace, silks, tea, tobacco and, of course, the brandy, which was so plentiful the entire parish seems to have been soaked in it. When a lugger landed her cargo, it was not uncommon for whole families, including the children, to keep up drunken orgies for three days and nights on end. Every receptacle in the district was needed to hold the spirit. As Catherine Carswell (1879 – 1946) related in her biography of Burns, there was one farm where no water-jug remained unfilled and the sodden servants would boil the breakfast porridge in proof brandy.

There was certainly excitement in these new scenes and experiences found in Kirkoswald by the bard, who had also been released from the drudgery of day to day toil on an 18th century farm. The riot and drunkenness in the parish must have been mind boggling for the young naive Burns. So frequent was drunkenness, even on the Sabbath, that the Kirk session enacted that no inn-keeper should sell on that day more than two pints of ale to a company of three persons. It is also reported that the vice of adultery was prevalent.

One incident alone illustrates the magnitude of the problems caused by smuggling and debauchery. The Kirkoswald Kirk Session, convened in October 1764, accused Samuel Brown (uncle of Burns) of smuggling on the Lord's Day. The elders were more concerned with the violation of the Sabbath than with the breaking of the law. Brown maintained that he had been in church that day, before going down to the shore to watch a Manx vessel. It proved a protracted affair and the Session were still dealing with it in July 1765 when forty-eight smugglers were hauled up for Sabbath-breaking. The deposition in this case mentions various individuals taking away ankers and casks from a Manxman. Among the four dozen smugglers admonished were Brown and several members of the Niven family. 11 As all his relatives appear to be entrenched in the trading of contraband, it is no great step to consider that during his time there, Burns would have been actively involved in the nefarious business of smuggling.

It is not surprising, given the above, that lines 20 to 28 of the poem concerning Tam's drinking pals were written. In fact it seems that Tam was not the worst offender concerning drink in comparison with the times.

It is not known exactly how long Robert spent in the area but it was around ten or eleven weeks. It is probable that he spent the summer term at school there, July till September, which is confirmed by the mention in the letter to Dr Moore when he mentions the sun entering Virgo (23 August). The choice of Kirkoswald was due to the 'noted school' mentioned in the letter and the availability of lodgings.

The 'noted school' was under the charge of Hugh Roger (1726-97) who was something of a self-taught genius. Hugh Roger was the son of John Roger and Mary Bodan, who rented the farm of Thomaston Mill near Kirkoswald.

Roger was seen to be inclined to the acquisition of knowledge from an early age and was his own teacher. He learned to form his letters and numbers on the beach adjoining the farm and as a young man he applied for a vacancy as the parish schoolmaster which he attained. He added to the scanty revenue this post produced by becoming a land surveyor and giving private tuition in advanced mathematics. He attained distinction as an instructor, and as a consequence the sons of those with rank were boarded with his family. Among his other pupils were the poet Sir Gilbert Blane and Sir Andrew Cathcart the noted physician.

In his early days Roger lacked proper premises and the school was a small apartment leased for a rent of one guinea per annum. He lived in a cottage of two apartments with small attics, and it was in the parlour of this house that Burns was taught. The site is marked by a commemorative plaque on the wall of the building, now operating as Souter Johnnie's Inn, Main Road, Kirkoswald, directly opposite the entrance to the cemetery.

Whilst not incredibly interested in mathematics, Robert would have been keenly aware of the cost to his father to send him to the school and would likely have made the most of his time there.

Souter Johnnie's Inn Kirkoswald

Ballochneil Cottage A77

While in Kirkoswald, Robert lodged at Ballochneil Farm with the Niven family and his maternal uncle Samuel Brown.

Ballochneil Farm and Mill no longer exist but were situated on the east side of the A77, just over a mile south of Kirkoswald behind the existing cottage of the same name.

Samuel Brown, born February 1739, was the half brother of Burns' mother and was a farm labourer who worked for Robert Niven, a farmer and miller. Samuel fell in love with the farmer's daughter Margaret and was brought before the Kirk Session on a charge of antenuptial fornication (sex before marriage) in April 1765. The couple married soon after. The marriage produced only one daughter Jenny who was immortalised by Burns in his poem 'Hallowe'en'. The Brown family lived in a single apartment outside the mill, so it is unlikely that Burns would actually have shared their accommodation. 12

Robert lodged with the Niven family in the farmhouse, sharing the attic bed of John Niven. It has been asserted that this John Niven was also a schoolmate of Burns, but this is not the case as John was already 21 when Burns came to stay. The classmate was Willie Niven of Maybole, who was slightly younger than Burns and lodged at the school with Roger. His father David Niven was a prosperous shop-keeper in Maybole and was the younger brother of the above mentioned Robert Niven. 13

Willie Niven, whilst younger than Burns, was much more alert and aware of his environment. It was Willie Niven who advised Burns that it was customary on enrolling at the school to take the schoolmaster to a tavern for a refreshment. It was thus that Burns was initiated into the ways of ale houses. Roger's favourite Howff was the Leddies House operated by Jean and Anne Kennedy, of which there is more later.

Willie and Robert became firm friends and spent all of their free time that summer together. Each Saturday, when the schooling was over, the pair would walk the four miles to Maybole to spend the weekend at Willies home above the shop. They spent a great deal of their time

together discussing theology, philosophy and other such deep subjects, examining all they knew of life.

In due course, they hit upon the plan of holding debates or arguments and involved a number of the other boys in their class. This came to the attention of Hugh Roger, who decided to nip this practice in the bud. One day Roger began commenting sarcastically to Burns and Niven about what he had heard of this practice. He told them that he had heard they had become great debaters, and thought they were competent to settle affairs of importance which wiser heads left well alone. The pupils laughed heartily at this sarcasm, which needled Niven into making the reply that he thought Roger would be pleased they were trying to improve their minds. This led to the contest of argument between Burns and Roger on the question "Whether it is a great general or a respectable merchant the most valuable member of society", which Burns won with pointed advocacy. 14

In early July, as the Kirkoswald Fair approached, Robert and Willie decided to organise a dance in one of the village pubs. The initial suggestion was made by Burns, and Niven readily agreed with the event taking place with 'the requisite music being supplied by a hired band.' Around a dozen couples took part and at the end of the evening, the tavern bill came to 18s 4d, perhaps this was 'the large tavern bill' Robert refers to in his letter to Dr Moore. In any event it was discovered that almost everyone present had no cash whatsoever apart from Niven who had half a crown (2s 6d) and another youth who had a groat (4d). Willie had to approach the landlord and induce him into accepting this small sum on account, with the promise of payment of the remaining 15s 6d at some later date. Willie took it upon himself to work off this debt and did it in some measure by selling pens and stationary to his classmates, having obtained them at cost from his father. 15

The outcome of this sojourn was that Burns saw life in the raw for the first time, made good friends and met most of the characters he subsequently used in the poem which put Kirkoswald on the map for many tourists.

Some of the characters from the poem are buried in the local village cemetery on Main Street and there is an instructional plate on the gate advising the sites of relevant graves.

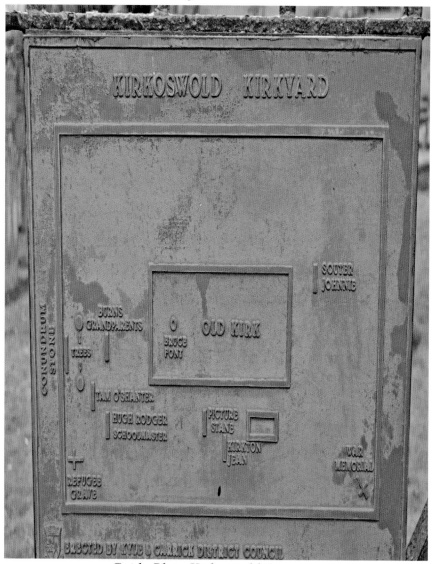

Guide Plate Kirkoswald Cemetery

62

the story of a tale

Tam and Kate

Tam has been wrongly identified in various publications as Thomas Reid (1745-1823) who died in Lochwinnoch. This probably stems from an article in the Scots Magazine in September 1823, which reported on the death of Reid. The article does not contain any evidence to support the assertion and where the idea originates is unknown.

Robert Graham was a farmer at Douglastown, Culzean Estate, near Kirkoswald. His landlord was Sir John Kennedy the second Baronet of Culzean, and both Sir John and his wife Jane (nee Douglas) thought well of Robert.

Lady Kennedy called by chance on Robert Graham when his wife was well advanced in pregnancy and the promise was made to her that, in commemoration of her visit, the expected child, boy or girl, would be named after her. A son was born and in honour of Lady Kennedy was named Douglas. 16

Douglas Graham, who would undoubtedly become the model for Tam o' Shanter, was baptised on 6 January 1738 according to the Kirkoswald Parish Register. He trained as an agriculturist and later obtained the lease of Shanter farm on the Carrick shore. He also later rented the farm of Laigh Park which is in the same area.

In 1766 he married Helen, daughter of John McTaggart tenant farmer at Hogstoun in Kirkoswald Parish. Helen is described as having an irascible temperament and her neighbours considered her to be eccentric and excessively whimsical. She had two brothers who were also considered to be rather odd. Helen was considered to be a superstitious shrew of a woman but this might be slightly unfair as most of the populace of the time would be superstitious to some degree or other.

Douglas and Kate had a family of five sons and one daughter. John, the eldest son, died aged 18 and is buried with his parents. Robert, the second son, led a chequered career, engaging in contraband and David the youngest son worked the farm with his father, later leasing Polcardoch Farm at Ballantrae.

63

Helen died in 1798, and Douglas died in 1811, so both would still be alive when the poem was published but there is no written record of their view on the poem.

Mrs Finlay of Helensburgh, who was the daughter of John Niven of Ballochniel, knew Douglas Graham in her childhood and described him as 'a fine looking old man, with a sanguine complexion; he wore a wig, and talked humorously.' 17

In addition to being a farmer, Douglas Graham was also a dealer in malt which meant travel to the market at Ayr on a regular, if not quite daily basis.

Both Douglas Graham and his wife Helen are buried in Kirkoswald cemetery, and the inscription on their headstone reads;

"Erected by Douglas Graham and Helen, his wife, in memory of their son John Graham, who died December 10, 1785 aged 18 years. Also Helen McTaggart, who died 2nd December, 1798, aged 56 years. Also Douglas Graham, who died February 14th 1811 aged 72 years."

Headstone of Douglas and Helen Graham

Why Tam?

The first Thursday in July 1775 was the day of the Horse Fair in Ayr and was a school holiday in Kirkoswald. Willie Niven in the company of Robert Burns decided to go on a fishing trip.

Douglas Graham like most coastal farmers in the region kept a boat, ostensibly for fishing and gathering seaweed for fertiliser but it was really to dabble a little in the notorious trade of smuggling. As would his neighbours, he co-operated in the movement of contraband goods for life's little luxuries.

The boat owned by Douglas Graham was the 'Tam o' Shanter' with the name painted on the stern. Why Douglas Graham named his boat Tam is not known or recounted in any contemporary note.

Robert and Willie decided to "borrow" the 'Tam o' Shanter' for their fishing expedition but all did not turn out well. The Chambers – Wallace edition 'Life and Works of Robert Burns' recounts the circumstances as cited by Reverend Charles Rogers;

'but, when they had moved some distance from the coast, they were assailed by a strong gale from the east. Such a gale implied danger, but when Niven proposed that they should steer shoreward, Burns objected, jocularly remarking that he not abandon his purpose, though the breeze should prove strong enough to blaw the horns aff the kye. At length he yielded to the advice of his more experienced, and reaching the shore, they affected a landing with some difficulty.'

Some local traditions have it that the boat was beached at the Dipple, which is just south of Maidens, around where the alginate factory stands today, and others report that the beaching was nearer to Shanter Farm. Wherever the landing point, both boys made their way to Shanter Farm for shelter, arriving thoroughly soaked by their adventures. Both boys would be well known to the Graham household and would, as a consequence, be made welcome there.

On arrival they discovered that Douglas Graham was off to Ayr and the Horse Fair, and they spent the evening in the company of Mrs Graham.

Helen Graham was reported to have a querulous temper and known to speak rashly and had expected Douglas to have returned by early evening. He failed to appear. She enthusiastically told the boys that some day he would fall into the river Doon in an intoxicated stupor and be found drowned. She included in her denunciation her husband's friend Johnnie Davidson (Souter Johnnie) who had accompanied Douglas to market in order to purchase leather for soles of shoes he was making.

On the return journey home, Robert remarked to Willie Niven on the' wanton censures' of the gudewife.

The Hidden Players

The two main actors in this feast of poetry often go unrecognised in the wake of Tam and all his cronies but to ignore them would be to fail to understand the main thrust of the tale.

Every bit as important to the poem as Tam is Satan, and perhaps even more crucial is the role of the narrator, the story teller.

Satan, the Devil, Auld Nick, Clootie or whatever he named him, Burns was certainly spellbound by him.

Burns first poetic brush with Satan comes in the 'Address to the Deil', composed during the winter of 1785-86, which Burns precedes by a quote from Milton;

O Prince! O Chief of many throned pow'rs
That led embattl'd seraphim to war

Address to the Deil has a number of verses and points that are relevant to Tam o' Shanter, but the use of Milton by Burns is the first hint of his infatuation with Satan in his works. On 11 June 1787 Burns wrote to James Smith and included this line:

'Give me spirit like my favourite hero, Milton's Satan,' and then he goes on to quote from Paradise Lost.

On 18 June 1787 he wrote to William Nicol saying:

'I have bought a pocket Milton which I carry perpetually about with me, in order to study the sentiments – the dauntless magnanimity; the intrepid, unyielding independence; the desperate daring, and noble defiance of hardship, in that great Personage, Satan.'

He discussed this liking for Milton's Satan with Agnes McLehose (Clarinda) who was a strict Calvinist and this positive reference to Satan must have upset her. Burns tries to defend his position in a letter written to her on 5 January 1788 when he states;

'My favourite feature in Milton's Satan is, his manly fortitude in supporting what cannot be remedied – in short, the wild broken fragments of a noble, exalted mind in ruins. – I meant no more by saying he was a favourite hero of mine.'

It appears from the circumstances that Burns saw the Satan created by Milton as what Hollywood would now term an 'anti hero'. Whatever the case, he was certainly fascinated by the Devil and, excluding Tam o' Shanter and Address to the Deil, goes on to refer to Satan by name in over 80 other poems and songs.

Address to the Deil is formed in three parts by Burns. The first is an invocation of the Devil by Burns using humour, the second relates the works and doings of Satan and lastly, a satirical farewell. In the middle section Burns goes on to describe many of the devilish manifestations he later uses in Tam o' Shanter, such as warlocks, withered hags, kelpies and spunkies. There is no doubt the poem is designed by Burns to use the Devil for comic effect, but it still reinforces his awareness of the evil satanic practices and confirms the appeal of Satan to him. Four years later, Burns has the Devil make a star appearance in his epic narrative and, in some academic minds, Satan is the creative energy behind the work.

The story is told by the narrator who is, of course, Robert Burns and it is not until line 13 at the start of the second paragraph that we are introduced to Tam himself.

It is the narrator who dictates the pace of the poem, giving it energy where necessary and, probably more importantly, giving it pause when dramatic effect is needed. It is the narrator who philosophises and moralises and not our Tam, he is just the subject of the poem.

From the start, the narrator seems to take the position needed to tell his story, sometimes the average man, sometimes from the view of a cronie and on occasion as a man of some education and breeding. The very first thing done is to describe the scene and then Kate and her womanly ways. It is done so well that most readers of the poem can easily imagine Kate ranting on about Tam and his profligate ways and perhaps identify with the predicament Tam finds himself in.

As the poem continues, there is a description of the weather, the wild ride and all the evil happenstance along the way, and as the

circumstances change so does the position and voice of the narrator in order to add life to the story.

The narrator continues on to move between description of the hellish business on hand in Alloway Kirk and moralising on the evils of drink, the quality of women and the outcome of being so rash as to get involved with such devilish disciples.

Whilst the narration is done from differing points of view, it is a narrative not a duologue. It is a dramatic monologue and, if changes in perspective appear, they come from a single place, the mind of Robert Burns. The works of Burns are littered with examples of him role playing, Luath and Caeser come easily to mind, and that is why when the narrator slips into the mind of Tam, seeing the world from his point of view, we accept the outcome without remark. At times it also seems as if the narrator is becoming excited by what is happening and it is possible to identify with Burns' enjoyment in writing the piece.

Whilst he is invisible in the tale, the teller of this dramatic story is undoubtedly the star of the show.

The Rest of the Cast

The **Smith** who drank the profits from shoeing horses with Tam was John Niven of Damhouse of Ardlochan.

Towards the end of the 17th century several Niven brothers (originally Neven) from Monkridding and Brigend areas of Kilwinning Parish settled in the Girvan area. The Niven family had done well over the previous hundred years and each would have had sufficient means to establish themselves in the new area. 18

One of the brothers, John Niven, invested his savings in stocking a farm in the vicinity of Girvan. His son James left home to take up tenancy at Ardlochan in the parish of Kirkoswald, and it was his oldest surviving son (two died young) John who settled as the blacksmith at Damhouse of Ardlochan.

John Niven, blacksmith, became well known for his introduction of wheeled carts of his own design and manufacture. During Burns' time by far the commonest means of transport was by pack or drawn sled. Carts were new, having only just being introduced. John Niven introduced wheels that rotated on a fixed axle, which would have been revolutionary at the time.

There is not much further known of John Niven and nothing that would allow us to have an opinion on his personal habits or behaviour. It could be a fair assumption, given the place and the time, that most working men would have enjoyed alcoholic refreshment on occasion, but whether or not Mr Niven would have drunk to the extent suggested by Burns is a matter of conjecture.

His son, Robert, became a miller at Ballochneil farm.

The identity of the **Miller** is not as clear cut with two individuals identified as possible.

Robert Niven, son of John, rented the mill and farm at Ballochneil which is just over a mile south of Kirkoswald on the banks of the Milton Stream (Corriston Burn). Robert married Margaret Ross. Her

first daughter was also named Margaret and, as is described earlier in Background on the Characters, after a colourful courtship, married Samuel Brown, a brother of Robert Burns' mother.

Samuel was employed on the farm as a labourer and he and Margaret occupied a single apartment next to the farm house.

Both of these individuals, Robert Niven and Samuel Brown, have been variously identified as the *Miller* in the tale.

Whilst it is possible the poet used Samuel Brown, his uncle, the evidence of the verse does not support this. The lines 23 and 24 are quite clear;

That ilka melder, wi' the miller,
Thou sat as long as thou had siller;

This verse is telling the reader, that after grinding, the miller and Tam sat and drank the proceeds. There is no doubt Samuel Brown enjoyed a drink, as his smuggling adventures would testify to, but he would not have gained the payment from milling corn. Brown was employed as a farm labourer earning, at best, £3-£4 per annum. The owner of the mill however, would be in a position to drink the profits of milling a melder of corn.

It is for this reason that the *Miller* was in all probability Robert Niven, son of John the *Smith*.

Another link to strengthen the relationship between the Miller and Tam could be found on the next farm down from Ballochneil, Laigh Dalquhat, which was the neighbouring farm when Burns resided there in 1775. Laigh Dalquhat was farmed by a Mr McTaggart, who was the brother-in-law of Douglas Graham. Whether Douglas Graham would pass the time with the Niven family when visiting their next door neighbours is unknown, but it is a strong possibility.

At some time after Tam o' Shanter was published, Robert Aiken, the Ayr lawyer and great patron of Burns, sent Robert Niven a manuscript copy of the poem. It has been reported that Niven read the poem to Douglas Graham and asserted that he, Graham, was the hero of the piece. Graham was unmoved by the striking descriptions of his activities, merely retorting that it was 'a parcel o' lees, for I never owned a grey mare, or one named Meg – or ony kind o' beast without a tail.'

Kirkton Jean was Jean Kennedy of Kirkoswald. Jean was born at Crossraguel in 1738 and was one of the daughters of Alexander Kennedy and Jean Aird. With her sister Anne she operated a small inn at Main Street Kirkoswald known as 'The Leddies House'. 19

Gravestone Jean Kennedy

The sisters occupied a fair social status in the village, enjoying unblemished fame and were usually described as the Leddies. In lowland Scotland any village in which the parish church was situated was known as the 'Kirkton', hence the naming of Jean by the poet.

The lines in the poem were published thus:

That at the L——d's house, even on Sunday,
Thou drank wi' Kirkton Jean till Monday.

As can be seen in the Kilmarnock Manuscript Burns tried to change Leddies for better rhyme to L——d's's but this was later abandoned

for a much improved rhythmical half-quibble. The only issue with the published version of L——-d's House is that over the years many have taken the abbreviation to mean Lords House, thinking of a church.

Local traditions have it that both Jean and Anne Kennedy were not the most attractive of women, and in order to get them off his hands their father thought up a cunning plan. He was of the opinion that by establishing them as owners and operators of an alehouse that they would be much more appealing as a catch for the men of the district. Whatever the reason, by being the publican at Kirkoswald in 1775, Jean has become immortalised in verse by one of the world's great poets.

Souter Johnnie was based on John Davidson of Glenfoot whom the poet would have known well.

There has also been the assertion that the character of Souter Johnnie was based on another shoemaker named John Lachlan or Laughton. Lachlan/Laughton was a shoemaker from Ayr who died in 1819 and is buried in Alloway Kirkyard. After his death the Scots Magazine September issue read "Died lately, John Lachlan, shoemaker in Ayr, known as an intelligent, lively and facetious companion. He was better known by the epithet of 'Souter Johnnie' by which title he is immortalised by Burns in his exquisite poem of 'Tam o' Shanter.'" Just where the evidence to support the printed claim arises is not known but the weight of other evidence and facts strongly supports the identity of the Souter to be John Davidson.

John was the son of Bryce Davidson who occupied a cottage at Jameston Farm and was born in February 1728. It was said that he inherited his father's love of sacred knowledge leading him to spend a portion of his first earnings as a cowherd on the book by Thomas Boston, 'Human Nature In Its Fourfold State'. This volume has been preserved and is an heirloom of the Davidson family today.

Davidson took up the trade of shoemaking, hence being known as a souter, which he plied from Glenfoot of Ardlochan, which was close by Shanter Farm.

On 31st July 1763, John married Anne Gillespie another native of the district. In her early life, Anne entered the service of Gilbert Brown, the maternal grandfather of Robert Burns. She served the Brown family at Craigenton whilst Agnes Brown, mother of Burns, resided there. Agnes had a high regard for Anne and encouraged her son to visit her and her husband at Glenfoot in later years. During these visits Burns occasionally also met Douglas Graham and became aware of the friendship that existed between Douglas and John Davidson.

However, the Souter who was not averse to social enjoyments was said to be of strictly sober habits. Given this, Burns must have been exercising his very active imagination to describe him as drouthy and drinking with Tam for weeks on end.

Mr Mathew Porteous, a printer in Maybole, made Davison the subject of a poem 'The Real Souter Johnnie' published in 1858. In verse he describes Davidson:

He was a gash wee fodgel body,
Stood on his shanks baith tight and steady;
As gleg's a hawk, as teuch's a wuddie,
Had gabby skill
To crack a joke, wi' wit aye ready
Out ower a gill.

Davidson was reputed for his quick wit, jests and sayings. One such saying came about when he was asked if his craft of shoe making might disappear in the future as new discoveries and technologies manifested, and he replied "My craft will continue so long as calves are born with heads, and bairns are born barefute." [20]

He took snuff regularly and his mull, a round wooden snuff box, is exhibited in the Burns Monument in Edinburgh.

In 1785 John Davidson built a cottage in Main Street Kirkoswald which he moved into with his family, and it was here he continued his trade.

Souter Johnnie's Cottage

John and Anne had a family of 2 sons and 3 daughters. His elder son, Mathew, followed his father into the family trade of shoemaking, taking over the business in due course.

The cottage stayed in the Davidson family until 1920. It was then handed over to a committee who oversaw its restoration, funded by Sir John Richmond of Blanefield, before passing to the National Trust for Scotland, who operate it as a museum. It is open between 1 April and 30 September from Friday to Tuesday, 11.30 am to 5 pm and is well worth a visit if you are in the area. Parking is no problem and the cottage is distinguished by its thatched roof, other cottages that were originally thatched have since been slated. The entrance is around the back, and this gives access to a nice recreation of village life at the end of the 1700s.

John Davidson died on 30th June 1806 and is buried in Kirkoswald Cemetery where you can find his gravestone clearly marked.

Gravestone John Davidson

The individual who inspired **Nannie,** the witch, has been identified as Katie Steven or Stein. 21

Katie lived alone at Laighpark, in the parish of Kirkoswald. Laigh Park Farm is also near to Ballochneil where Burns resided during his time in Kirkoswald. Katie lived in a cottage on the farm and was well known locally. It is another irony of this tale that Douglas Graham, model for Tam, also farmed Laigh Park at one stage.

Katie lived her whole life in the parish and died there in 1816. She enjoyed the reputation of being a good fortune teller and was a favourite guest among her neighbours. Again, there is no direct evidence to confirm it but it is feasible that she would have entertained the Niven family whilst Burns was living on their farm.

However, as with all such women in her day, others who knew her less well considered her to be a witch who was addicted to and practiced the black arts, so wonderfully described in the poem. She was also reputed to be an active accomplice of the Carrick smugglers. Given the fact that most of the population, including the relatives of Burns, were also involved in contraband running it would be no great surprise to find Katie in the thick of it. More to the point was the allegation that she was a receiver of such illicit goods making her one of the districts prime candidates in that trade Scots Law lovingly calls 'Reset'.

Whatever the truth she was a colourful character and if the poetic description given by Burns is in anyway accurate, she must have been a most attractive woman.

The Haly Table

It is often assumed by readers of the poem that the old Scots word 'haly' means holy. It can be used in such a way but in the context of Tam o' Shanter the opposite is the case.

Haly or halie is a euphemism for the devil and references to it can be found extensively in the 17th century. The word arises from the term 'halie mans lay' which describes a piece of land left untilled as an act of propitiation to the devil. In 1649 the following text by Crammond illustrates the point;

"Alwayes it wes found that ther wes some piece of land in this parochme unlaboured, called the halie mans ley, dedicated to superstitious uses."

The word is used by Burns in the poem as an adjective to describe the table and as a consequence the items on it. This gives a more sinister tint to items which are already dark and foreboding and, to some extent, changes the reader's perception of them. By understanding they are placed on the table to appease the Devil, the reader begins to grasp their significance in the hellish scene before Tam's eyes. In using the term, Burns is compounding the horror and ensuring the reader does not interpret anything comic in the actions of the witches and warlocks cavorting to the tune played by Satan. The reader now knows this is a satanic sect in full swing and so he deliberately increases the shock and disgust of the scene. The horrors on the table are the offerings made by witches as evidence of their devotion to their master's service. The offerings would be made to Satan before the end of the dance.

'A murderer's banes in gibbet airns;' line 132

A gibbet is a gallows type structure from which the dead bodies of criminals were hung for public display in order to deter future criminals from their activities. The practice was also known as 'hanging in chains'. The use of gibbets led to many towns and cities, including Edinburgh, having a Gibbet Street or other such nomenclature on local places.

The use of gibbets, or hanging of carcasses after execution can be traced back to the bible, and the Book of Joshua Chapter viii tells of Joshua ordering the carcass of the King of Ai to be hung from a tree. The procedure was common throughout Europe up to midway through the 19th century and in Scotland it is recorded that the infamous Deacon Brodie was required to improve the gibbet to be used for his execution whilst he was awaiting that fate in the Old Tollbooth Prison.

It was normally used on only the most serious crimes such as murder, treason, highway robbery and piracy. The bodies were often left till the clothes rotted and they decomposed, at which time the bones would be scattered. In England, in 1752, the Murder Act was passed which regularised the use of gibbets, empowering judges to use them in cases of murder.

The airns or irons were the chains or cage used to hang the criminal from the gibbet.

It is possible that Burns consciously places a murderer in his gibbet as the first thing on the table to ensure the 18th century reader would know how serious this demonic sect of witches and warlocks was about their business and pleasing their master, the Devil.

What is interesting is that the town gibbet of Ayr was situated directly on the route Tam would have taken on his ride but is not mentioned as part of the journey. The traditional site of the town gibbet was in what is now Midton Road, Ayr. Perhaps the use of gibbet irons containing a body in conjuction with the witches was of more use to the narrative. One can only guess.

The bones of the murderer would also be of value to the witches in the making of potions and poisons as they were considered to have a magical potency and evil charms. There are many accounts of graves being plundered by witches who would cut off body parts such as the fingers, toes and nose from the corpses to make powders for evil purposes.

'Twa span lang, wee, unchristen'd bairns;' line 133

The view has been articulated that Burns was referring to his own twin girls born on 3 March 1788, one of whom died on 10 March 1788, and the other on 23 March 1788. This probably stems from the notion that the tragedy of the loss of the twins would still be fresh in the mind of Burns when only fourteen months later he agreed with Captain Grose to write the poem.

Whilst this is a possibility it is unlikely. With all his children, Burns ensured they were baptised within a day or two of their birth and as a consequence it must follow that the twin girls did not die unblessed by the church. This being the case, the poor children could not be the inspiration for this line.

What is much more likely is that the use of two unchristened babes was a deliberate and direct reference by Burns to the beliefs allegedly held by witches.

Infant corpses were valuable to witches and this is reported by Reginald Scot in his Discoverie of Witchcraft 1584 when he says *"if there be anie children unbaptised, or not garded with the signe of the crosse, or orizons; then the witches may and doo catch them from their mothers sides in the night, or out of cradles, or otherwise kill them with their ceremonies'.* As late as 1720, the Witch of Calder confessed that she had given the Devil the body and head of her dead child (Chambers Domestic Annals of Scotland 1861).

What is most enlightening is the confession made by Helen Guthrie (Confession of Bargarran Witches) in 1661 that the witches of Forfar "dug up the body of an unbaptised infant and took several parts thereof, as the feet, the hands, a part of the head, and a part of the buttock, and they made a pie thereof, that they might eat it, that by this means they might never make confession of their witchcraft". 22

What was commonly accepted was that witches, by their beliefs and by entering the Demonic Pact with the Devil, were rejecting Christianity and were worshiping Satan as their master. Throughout all the witch hunting in Scotland and elsewhere in Europe, the first task was to ensure that the witches confessed to their 'sin' of devil

worship in order that their immortal soul could be saved for the glory of God, and to allow them passage to heaven.

It makes perfect sense that a witch, who worshiped Satan, would not wish to go to heaven but would desperately want to go to hell to be with their master whom they had worshipped in life. Any witch made to confess to the 'sin' of witchcraft would be saved in Christian terms. To avoid this terrible fate the witches would eat the flesh of the unchristened children in order to prevent confession under torture. As the child had never been hallowed in the presence of God and never spoken a word, the belief was that the consumption of their flesh would physically stop the words of confession being spoken.

A thief, new cutted frae a rape,
Wi' his last gasp his gab did gape; line 134

The image of a dead man with the hangman's noose still round his neck and the mouth hanging open is a particularly vivid picture of revulsion even in a day and age where public execution was still in vogue.

Five tomahawks, wi' blude red-rusted;
Five scymitars, wi' murder crusted; line 136

The number five is of significance in both these lines in relation to devil worship. A pentagram or pentacle, being a five pointed star drawn by straight strokes, features in many religious practices. The earliest use of the sign can be traced as far back as 3000 BC but the actual word originates in ancient Greece.

The pentagram is used as a symbol in many faiths including Christianity, Judaism, Taoism, Mormonism and Neopaganism, but when it is inverted it becomes a symbol of Satanism and Occultism. Heinrich Cornelius Agrippa (14.9.1486 – 18.2.1535), a lecturer at the University of Dole in France, perpetuated the popularity of the pentagram as a magic symbol. The upturned symbol, with two points pointing upward, was considered to be a symbol of evil and attracted sinister forces. When in such configuration the pentagram becomes the Flaming Star, the hieroglyphic sign of the black magic goat which can be drawn in the shape with the two horns pointing up and the beard pointing down.

During Satanic Rites to invoke the presence of Satan, it is an essential part of the process to inscribe the inverted pentagram in the air whilst reciting the Aspectual Invocations (words of summoning).

The weapons so gorily described would also have an immediate effect on the 18th century reader.

A tomahawk is an axe used by Native Americans and was well known throughout Scotland. It would have been considered as a particularly vicious and brutal weapon and it is not surprising it turns up on the table as a gift for Satan. The weapon and the blood thirsty actions of the owners were the stuff of legend in Scotland thanks to Indian Peter.

Peter Williamson, born in Aboyne in 1730, the son of a crofter ploughman fell afoul of a roving gang out to capture young men for indentured servitude, another name for slavery. In 1743 Peter and 78 other children were forced aboard the ship Planter bound for Virginia where he was sold to another Scot from Perth named Hugh Wilson who had also been kidnapped and sold in the same manner. During the French and Indian wars the French attempted to drive off British settlers by having them killed and scalped or captured by their Indian allies.

In 1754, Peter was captured by Delaware Indians, and during his captivity was tied to a tree and had his hands and feet burned by flaming branches but survived. Many of his fellow prisoners were not so lucky and during his captivity he saw many tortured and killed. He finally managed to escape his captivity and make his way back to safety. He travelled back to Britain in 1756, arriving in Plymouth, and decided to walk home to Aberdeen. During this time he also began writing of his experiences and as he travelled through York he managed to find sympathetic assistance in the publishing of a book that was his story. It sold a thousand copies in three weeks, providing him with funds and notoriety. In order to boost sales he would dress up as an Indian and do a 'war dance' to attract crowds and induce them to purchase his book.

Included in the contents of his book was the details of the child slavery trade in and around Aberdeen, and it was this that got him into trouble. He was arrested and convicted of libel for selling scurrilous and infamous material, for which he was imprisoned. On release he went to Edinburgh where he took action in the Court of Session which forced the slave dealers into a reluctant admission and in 1768 Peter was awarded £200 in damages and 100 guineas costs. All of this made his exploits, and the nature of the American Indian, household knowledge. He even inspired Fergusson to mention him in verse.

'This vacance is a heavy doom
On Indian Peter's coffee-room'

It is implausible that Burns would not be aware of these adventures and would fully appreciate the impact of blood covered tomahawks on the populace.

A scimitar is a sword with a curved blade and originates in the middle-east and has Arabic, Persian, Turkish and Indian versions. It was mostly used to fight from horseback and was used against the Christian Crusaders in the 11th and 12th century by the Saracens fighting for possession of Jerusalem. It also became the weapon of choice for pirates in the 17th and 18th centuries and, again, would have been well known to the average Scot. To have five of them crusted by murder is a deliberate ploy to add to the gruesome nature of the table.

A garter, which a babe had strangled; line 137

A garter was a narrow band of fabric fastened about the leg to hold up stockings. They would normally be only an inch or so in width and were usually made of heavy cloth or leather. In the 18th century they were usually tied below the knee to keep the stocking from slipping and they were sometimes adorned with ribbons or lace or small bells. Whilst in modern day terms the use of garters is mostly symbolic, brides for instance, they were commonplace in the 18th century. The garter also has roles in witchcraft.

A garter is worn by a Witch Queen as a symbol of rank. By tradition, the garter is prepared with green leather with a lining made of blue silk. There is one large, silver buckle on the garter, representing the Queen's own coven, with additional, smaller, silver buckles for each of the other covens under her authority. It is worn on the left leg, just above the knee.

Red garters were traditionally worn by a witchcraft coven Messenger. At the time of the persecutions, he would be sent out by the Priestess to advise members on meeting days and times. The red garters signified to others that he was genuine.

Pennethorne Hughes (author of Witchcraft 1952) states that when a tortured witch was likely to reveal others, he or she may be murdered in jail by the other witches to avoid further arrests and tortures. To prove that the murder had been done under those circumstances, a garter would be left tied loosely around the victim's throat. Such a potential informant would be known as a "warlock," meaning traitor. The case of John Stewart of Irvine in 1618 is one such example. John Reid, of Renfrewshire in 1696, is another.

Here we have Burns combining the innocent accidental death of baby with the infernal machinations of witches and their homage to Satan in an obviously appalling representation.

A knife, a father's throat had mangled,
Whom his ain son o' life bereft,
The grey hairs yet stack to the heft; line 140

To Robert Burns the thought of patricide, the act of killing one's father, must have been extremely abhorrent. This is probably why the knife used in such a crime is on the table in order to produce revulsion in the reader.

Burns deeply respected his father as can be evidenced in his Epitaph on my Ever Honoured Father:

O ye whose cheek the tear of pity stains,
Draw near with pious rev'rence, and attend!
Here lie the loving husband's dear remains,
The tender father, and the gen'rous friend;

The pitying heart that felt for human woe,
The dauntless heart that fear'd no human pride;
The friend of man – to vice alone a foe;
For ev'n his failings lean'd to virtue's side.
Wi' mair o' horrible and awefu',
Which even to name would be unlawfu'. Line 142

Burns is using the last two lines as a catch all to inspire further terror in the reader of the items on the table. After the descriptions given of the other items it bogles the mind to think what could be so terrible that it would be criminal to lay name to them.

With the exception of the deleted lines (discussed in Deleted Lines and Changes) viz:

Seven gallows pins, three hangman's whittles,
A raw of weel seal'd doctors' bottles (follows line 136)

and

Three Lawyers tongues turn'd inside out,
Wi' lies seam'd like a beggars' clout;
Three Priests hearts, rotten black as muck,
Lay stinking, vile in every neuk. - (follows line 142)

we cannot begin to determine what the poet is hinting at, but the overall impression left is a frightening abundance of obscenities.

Some Explanations on the Text

Throughout other chapters of this book, the terms and meanings of many of the actual words and phrases written in the poem are explained in context with that chapter. However this leaves a great many words and phrases which go unexplained and this chapter is an attempt to redress this issue.

What follows is a line or lines from the poem accompanied by an explanation on the line(s) of text.

When Chapman Billies leave the street (line 1). A chapman was a petty itinerant merchant or dealer or pedlar. The word originates in the 13th century and relates to anyone trading or selling in small portable goods. In addition, there was a common usage of the phrase *Chapman's drouth* which referred to a pedlar asking for a drink, and by implication something to eat along with the drink. The phrase *Chapman's law* relates to the practice of a publican allowing the chapman to trade in his premises without cost, on the understanding the company would buy drinks. The chapman dealt in small, easily transportable items such as knives and garters. Burns relates this in his other poem 'On Tam the Chapman'.

While we sit bousing at the nappy (line 5). The nappy or nappie was ale or liquor that was foaming, brisk, strong, rich and heady. It also applied to the container in which such drink was kept.

We think na on the lang Scots miles (line 7). A Scots mile was 1984 yards long, some 224 yards longer than an English mile. If you would like to walk one South Ayrshire Council created a measured Scots mile on the seafront at Ayr which is well signposted.

She tauld thee weel thou was a skellum (line 19). A skellum was a worthless fellow, a scamp, scoundrel or rogue.

A blethering, blustering drunken blellum (line 20). A blellum was an idle talking man.

That ilka melder wae the miller (line 23). A melder was the quantity

of grain a person would take to the miller to have ground at one time.

That in the L——-d's house even on a Sunday (line 27). It is often assumed by those doing recitations that L——d's house should be spoken as Lords house meaning a church. The actual reference is to "The Leddies House", which was a public house in Kirkoswald operated by the Kennedy sisters Jean and Ann. Jean Kennedy is the 'Kirkton Jean' in the following line. Kirkton is any village with a kirk in it. It is thought that the abbreviation to L——d's house was done by Burns to improve the rhythm of the piece. South Ayrshire Council erected a small plaque indicating the site of the pub in Kirkoswald on the A77 just before the graveyard.

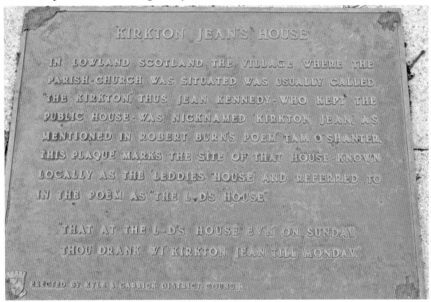

Plaque in Main Street Kirkoswald

Fast by an ingle, bleezing finely, (line 39). The principle meaning for an ingle was a domestic fire on a household hearth, or a fire used to heat a room of any kind. It was also used to describe burning material taken from a fire or a furnace.

Wi'reaming swats that drank divinely; (line40). Reaming in this sense means foaming. The use of the word drank is not literal, it means tasted. This descriptive term was widely used and common in 17th and 18th century English.

And at his elbow, Souter Johnny (line 41). A souter was a shoe maker or cobbler.

The natives of both Selkirk and Forfar are sometimes known as "Souters" due to the towns having a history of shoe manufacturing.

Care, mad to see a man sae happy, (line 53). The word care in this context is an Augustan abstraction meaning that the individual was disposed in an offhand and highly indecorous way. 23 In English literature, Augustan poetry flourished during the first half of the 18th century and the school included poets such as Alexander Pope and John Gay. The poems were all satirical in nature following from the fact that the term stems from George I, who saw himself as Augustus, and British poets picked up on this.

Or like the borealis race, (line 63). The Aurora or Northern Lights.

Wi' tippeny, we fear nae evil (line106). Tippenny was a weak beer sold at the cost of two pence per Scots pint, which was equal to two quarts.

Wi' usquabae we'll face the devil (line107). Usquabae is whisky.

Fair play, he car'd na deils a bodle (line 110). A bodle is variously described as a halfpenny or a farthing in assorted texts printed with the poem. A Bodle is, in fact, a copper coin of the value of two pennies Scots, equivalent to one sixth of an English penny. The origin of the term was alleged to be derived from a mint-master named Bothwell. This is unlikely as Cochrane Patrick's 'Records of the Coinage of Scotland' states '*no person of that name was ever associated with the Scottish Mint*'. Due to the slight value of the coin, Tam obviously did not care a great deal about the scene in front of him, unlike his horse which had more sense.

Warlocks and witches in a dance (line115). There are many references to witches dancing stemming from the 15th and 16th centuries. Traditionally, witches would dance in a ring or in more complex patterns back to back. There is also a relationship between witch dancing and fertility rites, these would be more obscene in nature. In

'The Dialogue of Witches' by Danaeus it is quoted "Witches frequently meet in or around a church. Satan calls them 'togither into a Diuelish Sinagoge, and that he may also understand of them how well and diligently they have fulfilled their office ... and who they have slain ... Then do they all repeat the oath which they have given to unto him, in acknowledging him to be their God, then fall they to dancing." This sort of knowledge regarding the behaviour of witches was commonly known and would have been passed to Burns from several sources. 24

Nae cotillion brent new frae France (line116). A cotillion is a type of patterned social dance, which originated in France in the early 18th century, becoming popular there for almost 200 years. It was originally made up of 4 couples in a square formation which developed as the years passed with more couples being added to the dance. The name stems from the French word cotillon – petticoat – which reflected the flash of petticoats as the partners whirled and turned.

But hornpipes, jigs, strathspeys and reels (line 117). These are all the names of dances with the hornpipe for a single performer, the strathspeys for two and the reel for two couples describing figures of eight. The reel is medieval in origin and the strathspey comes from the 17th century. Burns is describing a scene of multiple dancers in an almost feverish state, being driven by the music without any of the sophistication expressed by the cotillion.

There is good evidence for witches making use of the bagpipes in their dancing. At the Tranent coven in 1669, the piper played 'two favourite airs of his majesty (the devil)', and in the North Berwick coven in 1590, much the same was done.

A winnock-bunker in the east (line119). This is a bunker or sill beneath the small east window of the kirk. As is described earlier in the route Tam approached from the south along the Doon and this would have led him to the small window on the south side of the kirk. This window is set quite high in the wall, but as Tam was on horseback he would have been comfortably able to look in and see the window in the east wall, which is the wall that faces on the main road (B7024) today.

A winnock-bunker in the east

There sat auld Nick in shape of beast (line 120). Throughout the European traditions the Devil takes animal shapes, which is perhaps why the bull trapped in the kirk, as related earlier, has some relevance to the tale. However, Tam saw a dog which had been reported before in Scotland. The Devil at Auldearne (1662) states "though he had fine faculty for metamorphosis, sometimes appeared as a dog." There are reports that the wife of the warlock William Barton (c. 1655) saw him leading a coven in the Pentlands 'in the likeness of a rough tanny dog, playing a pair of pipes'. In Satan's Invisible World Discovered by George Sinclair published in 1685 a woman, Agnes Simpson of Keith, also reports seeing him as a dog. 25

To gei them music was his charge (line122). The Devil is sometimes a central figure or at the least a participant in the witch-dance, but to Scottish covens he often plays the piper. His affection for the pipes is recorded as early as the Dance of the sevin deadly Synnis by

William Dunbar (1460-1520).

In a Historical Account of Witchcraft in Scotland by C K Sharpe (1819) there is a report of a legend in Burns' own time that a Glasgow citizen was passing through the Cathedral cemetery at midnight, when he 'saw a neighbour of his own, lately buried, rise out of his grave and dance a jig with the devil, who played the air called *"Whistle o'er the lave o't"* on the bagpipe'. This struck the city with so much horror that the town drummer was sent through the streets the next morning to forbid anyone to play, sing or whistle the nefarious tune.

He screw'd the pipes and gart them skirl (line123). Turned the drones on the pipes to get them in tune and made them squeal.

And by some devilish cantraip sleight (line127). In modern language a cantraip is used to describe a trick or a piece of mischief, but in the 18th century the meaning related to witchcraft and was a charm, a spell or a magic incantation.

Each in its cauld hand held a light (line128. Burns uses the dead here to illuminate the scene for Tam to view the Haly Table, but light was essential at sabbats (the major festivals of the witch's year) for illumination and as part of the ritual. It was most important in the witch cult spring festival of Candlemass. In 1590, the North Berwick Coven is alleged to have met 'be nycht in the kirk' and the Devil 'preachit unto a great number of them out of the pulpit, having lyk leicht candles rond about him.' Another account of a meeting in Forfar Kirkyard says 'they daunced togither, and the ground under them was all fyre flauchter [fluttering flames]'. [26] As can be seen in the chapter Deleted Lines and Changes the Kilmarnock Manuscript has a deletion of two lines here, which is of significance in relation to this part of the poem.

They reel'd, they set, they cross'd, they cleekit (line147). The dancers took hands and whirled round in the reel and faced their partners. They then passed across the circle of the dance, linked arms and turned.

Till ilka carlin swat and reekit, (line 148). A carlin was an old woman more properly described as a crone and it can also mean a witch. Swat and reekit was to sweat and steam.

And coost her duddies to the wark, (line 149). To strip off their clothes and cast them down. The term duddies generally meant clothes that were ragged and tattered or the worse for wear.

Been snaw-white seventeen hunder linen (line154). A manufacturer's term for fine linen woven in a reed of seventeen hundred divisions.

But wither'd beldams auld and droll (line159). A beldam was a grandmother or general term for an older lady.

Rigwoodie hags wad spean a foal (line160). A Rigwoodie is the chain or rope or leather strap which crosses the saddle of a horse's harness to support the shafts of a cart, and is interpreted to mean durable or tough. It can also mean withered or wizened. Some interpretations on the term Rigwoodie suggest it means 'worthy of the gallows' and this originates from the construction of the word. 'Rig' is also the name used for a strumpet (prostitute) and 'woodie' refers to gallows or gallows tree, so when read backwards it means gallows strumpet. 27

To spean a foal is to drive it off the teat with fright. They must have been ugly indeed if one look would frighten a foal from feeding.

Lowping and flinging on a crummock (line161). A crummock is a shepherd's crook and this is being used to aid the dancers leaping about in frenzy.

For many a beast to dead she shot
And perish'd mony a bony boat (lines167-168). There are documented accounts of covens in Scotland using witchcraft to destroy animals and crops. Fergusson also relates the use of witchcraft in such a manner in his poem The Ghaists: A Kirk-yard Ecolgue;

'Ere that day come, I'll 'mang our spirits pick
Some ghaists that trokes and conjures wi' Auld Nick,
To gar the wind wi' rougher rumbles blaw,
And weightier thuds than ever mortal saw:
Fire-flaught and hail, wi' tenfauld fury's fires,
Shall lay yird-laigh Edina's airy spires

And shook baith meikle corn and bear (line169). This was the staple crop of the time oats and barley.

Her cutty sark, o' Paisley harn (line171). This short garment was underclothes for every day wear which, even among the gentry, was made of harn. Harn is coarse linen woven from the tow which flax throws off when it went through the hackle. The tow was often spun at home and so was cheap to produce. Nannies' harn was Paisley and therefore had been purchased making it much more costly.

Wi' twa pund Scots ('twas a' her riches) (line 177). At the Union of the Crowns in 1707, the Scouts pound was equal to a twelfth part of the pound sterling, or 1s 8d (about 8 pence in modern money). This means the cutty sark cost 3s 4d which is expensive when you consider that a serving girl would earn less than £2 sterling a year in the mid 18th century.

Even Satan glower'd, and fidg'd fu' fain (line184). The devil is gazing on and then hitching his shoulders in glee at the scene before him.

As bees biz out wi' angry fyke,

When plundering herds assail their byke; (lines 193-194). Fyke has a literal translation as fuss and the herds referred to were keepers of herds such as shepherds or cowherds.

As open pussie's mortal foes (line195). This is a hunting term meaning to give tongue when following the scent. The dog would have an open mouth and its tongue would hang out following the trail left by the departing hare.

Ah, Tam! Ah, Tam! Thou'll get thy fairin!
In hell they'll roast thee like a herrin! (lines 201 – 202). There was a belief that miscreants would be hung up in hell and dried out like fish. In the publication 'Scotch Presbyterian Eloquence Display'd' published in 1738 on page 138 there is a quote "take them up by the Heels, reest them in the Chimney of Hell, and dry them like Bervy Haddocks."

And win the key-stane of the brig (line206). It was well known in the time of Burns that witches, or other evil spirits, have no power to follow any poor soul they are pursuing beyond the middle of a running stream.

The centre of Brig O' Doon

the story of a tale

Whene'er to drink you are inclin'd,
Or cutty-sarks run in your mind,
Think, you may buy the joys o'er dear;
Remember Tam o' Shanter's mare. (lines 221-224). Here Burns issues advice with a warning about drinking and avoiding paying the price to the Devil. He has done similarly in previous works. In 'Address to the Deil' he writes:

An' now, auld Cloots, I ken ye're thinkan,
A certain Bardie's rantin, drinkin,
Some luckless hour will send him linkan,
To your black pit
But Faith! He'll turn the corner jinkan
An' cheat you yet

Written in a Day

There is a commonly held opinion among many Burnsians that the poem was written in a single day. The idea that this is the case stems from John Gibson Lockhart and Allan Cunningham.

Cunningham (1784-1842) was born at Dalswinton and his father was a neighbour of Burns. He was an author who edited '*The Works of Robert Burns'*, an eight volume set, published in 1834. It is not clear where he gained direct evidence of Burns creating the poem in a single day.

Lockhart (1794-1854) published a biography of Burns in 1828, but the accuracy of this work is extremely doubtful as Snyder (Franklin Bliss Snyder The Life of Robert Burns 1932) says in his review of Lockhart "The best that one can say of it today is that it occasioned Carlyle's review. It is inexcusably inaccurate from beginning to end, at times demonstrably mendacious, and should never be trusted in any respect or detail".

Lockhart reports 'The poem was the work of one day; and Mrs Burns well remembers the circumstances. He spent most of the day on his favourite walk by the river where in the afternoon; she joined him with some of the children. He was busy "crooning to himself", and Mrs Burns, perceiving that her presence was an interruption loitered behind with her little ones among the broom. Her attention was presently attracted by the strange and wild gesticulations of the bard, who, now at some distance, was agonised with an ungovernable access of joy. He was reciting very loud, and with tears rolling down his cheeks, those animated verses beginning:

Now Tam, O Tam, had they been queans (lines 151 to 158).'

Mr Lockhart avers that the above was quoted from a manuscript journal of Cromek. 28

Robert Hartley Cromek (1770-1812) was an engraver to trade who was born in Hull. He journeyed to Scotland in 1808 to gather

information on the life of Robert Burns and his works. The same year he published his Reliques of Burns, consisting of Original Letters, Poems and Critical Observations on Scottish Songs. He was able to speak with many individuals who had personally known Burns and one of these was Jean Armour Burns.

Cromek did report this to be the case but any assertion that this means the poem was written on that day is purely from Lockhart. James Kinsley relates that the work carried out by Robert Dewar MA, Professor of English Literature at University College, Reading suggests 'Burns found difficulty carrying forward this particular point' referring to lines 151 to 158.

Mrs Burns' account gives the time of year as autumn at the latest but is was November of 1790 before any hint of Tam o' Shanter is found.

Mrs Dunlop received her first version of the poem anonymously in November apparently as joke but not by accident. She wrote to Burns 'I waked this morning to read a piece which had no hand but one could have produced' and she then quotes in sequence:

Kings may be blest, but thou art glorious,
O'er all the ills of life victorious:
As bees fly home laden with treasure,
By thee the moment's winged with pleasure.
But pleasure will not always last;
They're like the rainbow in the blast:
Awhile it shows its lovely form,
Then vanishes amid the storm.
The wind blew as 't' would blawn its last;
The rattling showers rose on the blast,
Each in its cauld hand held a light.

Mrs Dunlop speaks of 'the little stars of imagination' within the poem, and it appears her last three are such beauties quoted out of context. The first eight lines are probably transcript and not done from memory of the draft of the lines 53-56. The draft of the poem was substantial as Mrs Dunlop also praises Burns's groups 'on the road and in the kirk, as well as at home and at the market'. However it was not a complete draft as she also asks 'why have you defrauded me of a sheet where I find a thousand beauties beside those marked? She also quotes 131-134 and line 140. 29

In reply Burns sent Mrs Dunlop a letter from Ellisland in November 1790 which contained the following:

'I am much flattered by your approbation of my "Tam o' Shanter which you express in your former letter; though by the by, you load me in that said letter with accusations heavy & many; to all which I plead, Not Guilty! – Your book is I hear, on the road to reach me. – As to Printing of Poetry, when you prepare it for the Press, you have only to spell it right, & place the capital letters properly: as to the punctuation the Printers do that themselves. –

I have a copy of my "Tam o' Shanter" ready to send you by the first opportunity; it is too heavy to send by Post.

I am ever, my dear Friend and honored Patroness,

Yours Sincerely
Robert Burns'

In a second letter from Ellisland, dated 6 December 1790, which accompanied the poem, Burns writes;

'After tasking you with the perusal of so long a poem [Tam o' Shanter] it would be Egyptian to burden you in addition with a long letter.'

In response to this Mrs Dunlop replies;

'I applaud the editor [of the earlier draft]. Had I not seen the whole of that performance, all its beauties could not have extorted one word of mine in its praise, notwithstanding you were the author.'

Whilst not very complimentary, it does indicate that the poem had been subject to change.

Perhaps the best indication that the poem took more than a day to write comes from Burns himself. He wrote to Mrs Dunlop (11 April 1791) "... I look upon my 'Tam o' Shanter' to be my standard

performance in the poetical line..... it also shew in my opinion a force of genius and a finishing polish that I despair of ever excelling."

Mrs Dunlop replied that this finishing polish was 'a little tarnished by the sweat and the smoke of one line which I felt a little too strong for me.'

The deletions and changes discussed in the next chapter also point to a poem that took some time to complete. It would appear from all the circumstances and evidence available that the poem was written over a few weeks if not months in 1790 but, whenever it was in fact produced, many would concur with the poet that it is his best work.

Deleted Lines and Changes

There were quite a number of deletions and changes to the poem before the published version, many of which are important and quite a number that seem on the surface to be superficial.

In terms of the deletions, the best known are the lines that follow from the 'haly table' after line 142 viz:

Three lawyers' tongues, turn'd inside out,
Wi' lies seam'd like a beggar's clout;
Three Priests' hearts, rotten black as muck,
Lay stinking, vile, in every neuk.

These lines were in all the manuscripts, and in the version published by Frances Grose, but were deleted from the poem in 1793 after Burns was in correspondence with A F Tytler. Alexander Fraser Tytler, later Lord Woodhouselee (15 October 1747 – 5 January 1813), was an Edinburgh lawyer who became Professor of Universal History at Edinburgh University. He was appointed Judge Advocate for Scotland in 1790 and wrote widely for the periodicals of the time being well known in Edinburgh social circles. He is best remembered for his quote on the Cycle of Democracy, made in 1770. Tytler took a keen interest in Burns and all his works and encouraged the poet to develop his narrative skills.

Burns wrote the 'Epistle to Mr Tytler of Woodhouselee, Author of a Defence of Mary Queen of Scots' in May of 1787 and mentions him again in the poem 'To William Creech'. It is probable that Burns met Tytler during his first visit to Edinburgh, perhaps through Creech.

Alexander Fraser Tytler had a proof sheet of Tam o' Shanter on 11 March 1791 and the following day sent a letter of criticism and encouragement to Burns viz;

'Dear Sir, - Mr Hill yesterday put into my hands a sheet of Grose's Antiquities containing a poem of yours, entitled Tam o' Shanter; A Tale. The very high pleasure I have received from the perusal of this

admirable piece, I feel, demands the warmest acknowledgements. Hill tells me he is to send off a packet for you this day; I cannot resist, therefore, putting on paper what I must have told you in person had I met with you after the recent perusal of your tale, which is, that I owe you a debt which, if undischarged, would reproach me with ingratitude. I have seldom in my life tasted of higher enjoyment from any work of genius than I have received from this composition; and I am much mistaken if this poem alone, had you never written another syllable, would not have been sufficient to have transmitted your name down to posterity with high reputation. In the introductory part, where you paint the character of your hero and exhibit him at the alehouse ingle, with his tippling cronies, you have delineated nature with a humour and naiveté that would do honour to Mathew Prior; but when you describe the infernal orgies of the witches' Sabbath and the hellish scenery in which they are exhibited, you display a power of imagination that Shakespeare himself could not have exceeded. I know not that I have ever met with a picture of more horrible fancy than the following;

Coffins stood round, like open presses,
That shaw'd the dead in their last dresses;
And, by some devilish cantraip sleight,
Each in it's cauld hand held a light

But when I came to the succeeding lines, my blood ran cold within me;

A knife a father's throat had mangled
Whom his ain son o' life bereft
The grey hairs yet stack to the heft

And here, after the two following lines, "Wi mair o' horrible and awfu'" &c., the descriptive part might have been better closed than the four lines which succeeded, which, though good in themselves, yet, as they derive all their merit from the satire they contain, are here rather misplaced among the circumstances of pure horror. The initiation of the young witch is most happily described – the effect of her charms exhibited in the dance on Satan himself – the apostrophe,

"Ah little thought thy reverend grannie!" – the transport of Tam, who forgets his situation and enters completely into the spirit of the scene – are all features of high merit in this excellent composition. The only fault it possesses is that the winding-up, or conclusion, of the story is not commensurate to the interest which is excited by the descriptive and characteristic painting of the preceding parts. The preparation is fine, but the result is not adequate. But for this, perhaps, you have a good apology – you stick to the popular tale.

And now that I have got out my mind and feel a little relieved of the weight of debt that I owed you, let me end this desultory scroll by an advice: You have proved your talent for a species of composition in which but a very few of our own poets have succeeded. Go on – write more tales in the same style – you will eclipse Prior and La Fontaine; for, with equal wit, equal power of numbers and equal naiveté of expression, you have a bolder and more vigorous imagination. I am, dear sir, with much esteem, Yours &c.,   A.F.T.'

Burns replied to this letter from Ellisland in April 1791 writing:
'Sir,

Nothing less than the unfortunate accident I have met with could have prevented my grateful acknowledgements for your letter. His own favourite poem, and that an essay in the walk of the muses entirely new to him, where consequently his hopes and fears were on the most anxious alarm for his success in the attempt; to have that poem so much applauded by one of the first judges, was the most delicious vibration that ever thrilled along the heart-strings of a poor poet. However, Providence, to keep up the proper proportion of evil with the good, which it seems is necessary in this sublunary state, thought proper to check my exultation by a very serious misfortune. A day or two after I received your letter, my horse came down with me and broke my right arm. As this is the first service my arm has done since its disaster, I find myself unable to do more than just in general terms thank you for this additional instance of your patronage and friendship. As to the faults you detected in the piece, they are truly

there: one of them, the hit at the lawyer and the priest, I shall cut out: as to the falling off in the catastrophe, for the reason you justly adduce, it cannot be easily remedied. Your approbation, Sir, has given me such additional spirits to persevere in this species of poetic composition, that I can bring these floating ideas to bear any kind of embodied form, it will give me an additional opportunity of assuring you of how much I have the honour to be, &c.,'

The letter from Tytler clearly illustrates the effect on people of the time that the horrors on the 'Haly Table' were intended to do by Burns. His remarks relating to satire detracting from this are agreed by Burns and it is here that he decides to remove them from the finished poem.

Burns wrote to Tytler again in December 1792, passing on manuscript copies of his works for editing so the poet obviously valued the opinion of Tytler who was, after all, an educated man well positioned in society.

Cunningham (allegedly with credibility) notes an anecdote where a lawyer is said to have criticised the passage after hearing Burns recite saying "Obscure Sir." And Burns replied "ye know not that language of the great master of your own art – the Devil. If you get a witch for a client, you will not be able to manage her defence." 30

In general terms, Burns had no great love of lawyers as is evidenced by his Epigram 'Lord Advocate' where he writes:

But what his common sense came short
He eked out wi' law, man

but the letter reproduced above negates this attitude in relation to Tytler.

Another deletion from the poem also occurs in the section relating to the items on the Haly Table. The Kilmarnock Manuscript shows two lines following line 136 with an inked line drawn through them and they were

Seven gallows pins; three hangman's whittles;
A raw o' weel seal'd doctors' bottles,

It is not known why these lines were deleted by Burns but one explanation could be that the articles were not sufficiently gory for the effect the poet was trying to create. Gallows pins were commonly referred to in ballads of the times. The pins were a part of the gallows construction and on occasion they were substantial pieces of the structure and the poor individuals being hung could be suspended from the pin. On other gallows the pin was merely a projection that held a rope and it is probably this latter size of object that could be placed upon the table. In terms of Tam o' Shanter, they would have been nothing bigger than large pegs.

A whittle is a Scots word with several meanings, including a knife. It refers to a sheath-knife or a carving-knife and is found extensively in Scots poetry of the 18th and 19th centuries. Burns uses the term in numerous other poems including The 'Authors Earnest Cry and Prayer', 'Ballad on the American War' and 'Epistle to John Goldie, In Kilmarnock'. He uses it on two occasions in 'Death and Doctor Hornbook' and again he links the knife to a doctor and medical paraphernalia;

'And then a doctors' saws and whittles,
Of a' dimensions, shapes and mettles,
A' kinds o boxes, mugs and bottles
He's sure to hae;
Their Latin names as fast he rattles
As A B C

Burns must have been of the opinion that surgical equipment and medical supplies were every bit as frightening to the populace as they were a comfort in times of illness or injury. Given the state of medical science in the mid 18th century this is not surprising.

The Kilmarnock Manuscript has another two lines deleted by ink line directly following line 128 viz;

The torches climb around the wa'
Infernal fires, blue bleezing a'

Again it is not known why he chose to remove these lines, and as they

are significant in terms of setting the scene in the Kirk, there must have been a substantive reason.

Light was essential at sabbats as part of the witches' rituals, as well as for illumination, but the cancellation of the above lines is an important detail. Witch candles are made from pitch which burns with a blue flame. Once again the poet demonstrates a keen knowledge of the finer details of witchcraft.

Robert Ainsley gave a manuscript of Tam o' Shanter to Sir Walter Scott and he noted that when Burns had recited the piece to him at Ellisland on 16 October 1790, when visiting there, two lines followed line 50;

The crickets joined the chirping cry,
The kittling chased her tail for joy

As this is part of the joyous evening festivities in the inn with the storm roaring outside, it does seem a rather incongruous feature. How Tam could have heard crickets chirping on such a night does seem inconsistent with the night's activities. Ainsley reports that this lapse into 'little circumstance' is out of tone and was justly abandoned.

There are a number of changes to individual words as can been seen in the Kilmarnock Manuscript at Appendix I. The Lochryan Manuscript, the Abbotsford Manuscript, The Alloway Manuscript and the Liverpool Manuscript also all show evidence of changes to the text. Most of these are for poetical effect or to polish the piece after receiving advice and criticism from friends such as Anna Dunlop. It should be noted in publications of the poem, line 85 is written as prudent cares and the word used in line 114 is vow. The Kilmarnock Manuscript uses *anxious* in line 85 and *wow* in line 114 as can be seen at Appendix I.

The only change, which is perhaps other than this, occurs at line 95 where he changes the word *tree* to *thorn*.

He is being very specific with this change that Mungo's mother used a hawthorn tree to hang herself. Perhaps this stems from his intimate knowledge of the area and there was actually a hawthorn tree at this spot. Or maybe, once again, it refers to his knowledge of Scots folklore and witchcraft.

Hawthorn is one of the sacred trees of Wicka and Witchcraft, being strongly associated with the festival or Sabbat of Beltane, May Day spring celebrations. In spell-craft the wood from the tree is used as a blessing or to ensure the power of the spell. The wood is an ideal medium for the construction of wands to be used in rituals for enhanced spiritual communications. Hawthorn is also one of the nine woods traditionally placed in the Wiccan or Witchcraft balefire, which is a ritual fire created without the use of metals.

In Gaelic Scots and Irish folklore, a Hawthorn tree marks the entrance to the 'otherworld' and is considered a portal to the realm of fairies.

the story of a tale

Influences

Throughout the history of literature, great writers have been influenced by many factors, including writers who have gone before them. It seems impossible that creative writing could happen in a vacuum without outside influences affecting the outcome of a piece. Many great literary figures of the past have identified their sources of inspiration and Burns was no different.

In the second half of the 18th century, access to written information was much more restricted than it is today and when a good book was read it was cherished either in actual possession or in the memory of the reader. Robert Burns was an avaricious consumer of the written word and had the ability to retain a great deal of what had been read. Throughout his poems and songs there are clear references to the works of other writers and to parts of The Bible.

What follows are the names of those who appear to have influenced parts of Tam o' Shanter, with a brief background on each and some evidence that Burns actually read their works. Thereafter the line from Tam o' Shanter is given in italics followed by the relevant work and lines of that author.

There are other possible influences indentified and published by others such as Otto Ritter, Thomas Crawford, James Kinsley, David Daiches and contemporary poet Robert Wilson that are not listed in this chapter. The reason for this is that no direct evidence could be found to suggest that the works of an individual had been read by Robert Burns. In many cases it is entirely possible, indeed probable, that Burns had read the work concerned but no direct connection could be found.

Robert Fergusson (5 September 1750 – 16 October 1774), born in Edinburgh and educated at St Andrews University, lived the bohemian life in Edinburgh and was first published in 1773. Despite a short life his poems were very influential, particularly so on Robert Burns. Burns speaks of Fergusson often in his correspondence and writes of him in several poems including 'The Epistle to John Lapraik' where he uses the line "Ill-fated genius! Heaven-taught Fergusson".

Perhaps the most obvious facet of the influence Fergusson had on Burns is manifested when Burns commissioned and paid for a headstone on the grave of Fergusson in Cannongate Kirkyard in Edinburgh.

When chapman billies leave the street,

From the poem Hallow-Fair line 28 reads 31

Here chapmen billies tak their stand

She prophesised that late or soon,
Thou would be found deep drown'd in Doon;
Or catch'd wi' warlocks in the mirk,
By Alloway's auld haunted kirk.

From the poem The Ghaists: A Kirkyard Ecologue lines 9 and 10 read 32

... the Greyfriars, where at mirkest hour,
Bogles and spectres wont to tak their tour

And at his elbow, Souter Johnny,

In his poem The Election, which influenced several of Burns' works including the Holy Fair, Fergusson introduces the character Souter Jock in the tenth verse 33

Weel lees me o' you, souter Jock!

Alexander Pope (21 May 1688 – 30 May 1744) a famous English poet best known for his satirical verse and his translation of Homer. When he died he was the greatest poet of his age but later poets, including William Wordsworth, were critical of his work. Lord Byron identified him as one of his chief influences and there is no doubt Burns was equally persuaded. When Burns wished to lavish praise of John Lapraik of Muirkirk in that fine work *Epistle to John Lapraik an old Scotch Bard* he wrote:

I've scarce heard ought described sae weel'
What gen'rous manly bosoms feel;

the story of a tale

Thought I, 'Can this be *Pope*, or *Steele*,
Or *Beatties* wark;'
They told me 'twas an odd kind chiel
About Muirkirk

There is no doubt that Alexander Pope and his works were read by Burns and influenced his own creations.

But to our tale; Ae market-night,

From the poem The Wife of Bath her Prologue line 328 reads 34

But to my tale:—A month scarce pass'd away,

The doubling storm roars through the woods.

From The Temple of Fame line 333 35

'Thro' the big dome the doubling Thunder bounds'.

The lightnings flash from pole to pole;
Near and more near the thunders roll;

From Odyssey 36

Then Jove in anger bids his thunders roll
And forky lightnings flash from pole to pole.

As bees biz out wi' angry fyke,
When plundering herds assail their byke;
As open pussie's mortal foes,
When, pop! She starts before their nose;
As eager runs the market-crowd,
When 'Catch the thief!' resounds aloud;
So Maggie runs the witches follow,

From Iliad 37

Meanwhile the troops beneath Patroclus care,
Invade the Trojans, and commence the war.
As wasps provok'd by children in their play
Pour from their mansions by the broad high-way. (lines 312 – 315)
Thus from the tents the fervent legion swarms,
So loud their clamours, and so keen their arms; (lines 321-322)

As when two skilful hounds the lev'ret wind,
Or chase thro' woods obscure the trembling hind; (lines 427-428)

So close, so constant, the bold Greeks pursue. (line 432)

Allan Ramsay (15 October 1686 – 7 January 1758), born in Leadhills, was a noted poet, playwright, librarian and wigmaker. His first volume of poems was published in 1721 and in 1731 a complete edition of his poems was printed in London. He also published Scots songs and wrote a number himself, including the words to The Archer's March for The Royal Company of Archers.

Due to his standing, Ramsay and his works would have been familiar to Burns and the poet quotes from Ramsay in his letters, in particular to Clarinda. It can also be proved conclusively that Burns had access to his poems. Dumfries and Galloway Council have in their possession a copy of the Poetical Works of Allan Ramsay. Inside the front cover there is an inscription which reads "From Mr James Gray to Mr William Dunbar 1780" which is followed by "And from him to his ingenious friend Mr Robert Burns the Bard of Ayrshire 1788."

William Dunbar met Burns in Edinburgh through Masonic contacts and they became firm friends. Burns mentions him often in his correspondence and Dunbar also presented Burns with a copy of Spencer's (Edmund Spencer 1552-1599) poems, a gift that was greatly treasured. With regard to the song Rattlin, Roarin Willie, Burns wrote "The last stanza of the song is mine; it was composed out of compliment to one of the worthiest fellows in the world, William Dunbar Esq., Writer to the Signet, Edinburgh, and Colonel of the Crochallan Corps, a club of wits who took that title at the time of raising the fencible regiments."

Wi' reaming swats that drank divinely;

From the poem Picture of an Honest Ale-Seller lines 31-34 38

She ne'er gae in a Lawin fause,
Nor Stoups a Froath aboon the Hause,
Nor kept down Tip within her Waw's,
But reaming Swats

the story of a tale

Evanishing amid the storm,- (The word evanishing is an aureate term. Aureate writing style was used commonly in 17th century in Scottish literature. It is a style of writing that is affected, pompous and heavily ornamented and was first used in 15th century writing in England, Scotland and France.)

From Gentle Shepherd 39

Cares evanish like a morning dream

Lest bogles catch him unawares:

From the poem Richy and Sandy lines 8-9 40

Or has some bogle-bo
Glowerin frae 'mang auld Waws gi'en ye a Fleg

By this time he was cross the ford,

Where in the snaw, the chapman smoor'd;
And past the birks and miekle stane,
Where drunken Charlie brak's neck-bane;
And thro' the whins and by the cairn,
Where hunters fand the murder'd bairn;
And near the thorn, aboon the well,
Where Mungo's mither hang'd hersel.

These calamities can also be attributed to witchcraft, as is evidenced again in Gentle Shepherd 41

"a catalogue of misfortunes blamed on Mause, including 'When Watie tint himsell amaist amang the snaw' and 'Bawsy shot to dead upon the green'."

There sat auld Nick in shape o'beast;

From the poem The Monk and the Millers Wife lines 251-255 42

Radmanthus Husky Mingo,
Monk-horner, Hipock, Jinko, Jingo,
Appear in Likeness of a Priest
No like a deel in Shape of Beast,
With gaping Chafts to fleg us a'

But Tam kend what was what fu' brawlie,

There was ae winsome wench and wawlie,

From the poem A Tale of Three Bonnets 43

She was a winsome wench and waly,
And cou'd put on her Claiths fu' brawly.

James Thomson (1700-1748) was born in Roxburgh and became a poet and playwright. He is best known for his masterpiece The Seasons and for writing the words to Rule Britannia. Burns quotes from Thomson's works in his letters on well over twenty occasions and mentions his abilities in a letter to Dr John Moore in 1787 saying 'where Thomson and Beattie have painted the landskip, and Littleton and Collins described the heart; I am not vain enough to hope for distinguished poetic fame.' This indicates that Burns was familiar with the works of Thomson and was influenced by them.

The Souter tauld his queerest stories;
The landlord's laugh was ready chorus;
The storm without might rair and rustle,
Tam did na mind the storm a whistle.

From the poem The Seasons, Winter, lines 89-93. 44

the cottage-hind
Hangs o'er the enlivening blaze, and tableful there
Recounts his simple frolic: much he talks,
And much he laughs, nor recks the storm that blows
Without, and rattles on his humble roof.

William Hamilton of Gilbertfield (1665 1751) was a minor Scots poet who influenced Burns greatly in many respects. Hamilton lived at Gilbertfield in Lanarkshire and, after spending time in the army, he became friendly with Allan Ramsay and both poets exchanged epistles. In his Epistle to William Simson in May 1785 Burns was envious of the ability of Hamilton and Ramsay when he wrote:

My sense wad be in a creel,
Should I but dare a hope to speel
Wi' Allan, or wi' Gilbertfield,
The braes o' fame

Or Fergusson, the writer-chiel,
A deathless name.

In what is now known as his autobiographical letter to Dr John Moore, written in 1787, Burns states 'The first two books I ever read in private, and which gave me more pleasure than any two books I ever read again, were, the life of Hannibal and the History of Sir William Wallace. .... while the story of Wallace poured a Scottish prejudice in my veins which will boil along there till the flood-gates of life shut in eternal rest.' This was the abridged and modernised version of Blind Harry's Wallace published in 1722 by Hamilton.

The minutes wing'd their way wi' pleasure:

From History of Sir William Wallace 45

Let wing'd with pleasure, the softest minutes flow
And lasting bliss no interruption know.

Samuel Johnson (1709-1784), an English author who was often referred to as Dr Johnston and made a lasting contribution to English literature as a poet. Buried in Westminster Abbey, Johnson has had a lasting effect on literary criticism being regarded as the only great critic of English literature.

The Greenland tale by Johnson, Aningait and Ajut, was published in Masson's Collection. Arthur Masson published 'A Collection of Prose and Verse, from the Best English Authors. For the Use of Schools' which was used by Burns in school as he writes to Dr Moore "I met with these pieces in Masson's English Collection, one of my school books." Johnson was well enough known and published in Scotland for Burns to have read his work and he mentions several works of Johnson on four occasions in his letters. What is certain however is that Burns was aware of Aningait and Ajut through his school book and studies.

Or like the rainbow's lovely form,
Evanishing amid the storm,-

From Aningait and Ajut 46

'What art thou, deceitful pleasure! but a blaze streaming from the north which plays a moment on the eye and then vanishes forever."

William Cowper (1731-1800), born in Hertfordshire was one of the most popular English poets of his time and greatly admired by William Wordsworth, Samuel Taylor Coleridge said he was "the best modern poet".

Burns wrote to William Dunbar from Ellisland in September 1788 and in this letter he says:

'.... accept of my thanks for your letter; your Cowper Poems, the best Poet out of sight since Thomson: ...' Having received a volume of Cowper poems from his friend Burns went on to write in another letter 'Is not The Task a glorious poem' referring to that work by Cowper.

That ance were plush, o' gude blue hair,

From the poem The Task 47

As yet black breeches were not, sattin smooth,
Or velvet soft, or plush with shaggy pile.

Reverend John Skinner (1721-1807) led a colourful life and was a pioneer song collector and composer of several well known ballads. Inspired by The Edinburgh Edition, he wrote to Burns enclosing his rhyming Familiar Epistle to Robie Burns The Plowman Poet, In His Own Style.

Burns replied to Skinner on 25 October 1787 from Edinburgh and included in the letter was the following:

' ... I had not the pleasure of paying a younger brother's dutiful respect to the Author of the best Scotch song ever Scotland saw – "Tullochgorum's my delight". ..... Your three songs "Tullochgorum" "John Badenyon" and "Ewie wi' the crookit Horn" go in the second number. I was determined, before I got your letter, to write to you, begging that you would let me know where the editions of these pieces may be found'

As bees biz out wi' angry fyke,
When plundering herds assail their byke;

the story of a tale

From the song The Monymusk Christmas Ba'ling 48

Like Bumbees bizzing frae a byke,
When herds their riggings tirr

Robert Sempill of Belltrees, Renfrewshire, (1595-1659) wrote the Life and Death of the Piper of Kilbarchan, also known as the Epitaph of Habbie Simpson. This poem became very important in the history of Scots literature as it resurrects an old verse form afterwards named 'Standard Habbie', from the title. It consists of six lines, the first, second, third and fifth lines have 4 beats and rhyme, while the fourth and sixth lines have 2 beats and rhyme. The stanza was elaborated on by Allan Ramsay and Robert Fergusson but it was most widely used by Robert Burn to such an extent it is sometimes known by the alternative title of 'Burns Stanza'.

Whilst no direct reference can be traced in the works or letters of Robert Burns referring to Sempill, it seems impossible that Burns would not be aware of the poem.

He screw'd the pipes and gart them skirl,

From Epitaph of Habbie Simpson 49

And at Horse-races many a day,
Before the Black, the Brown and Gray,
He gart his pipe when he did play,
Both skirl and skried:
Now all such pastim's quite away
Sen Habbbie's dead.

An anonymous ballad arising from the oral traditional and later collected by **Thomas Percy** and published in 1765 which may have influenced Tam o' Shanter was The Ballad of Chevy Chase. This ballad was widely circulated in the 17th and 18th centuries on broadsheets and was well known in Scotland.

In 1435 or 1436 Percy Earl of Northumberland led a party of 4000 men into Scotland on a raid and was met in the Cheviot Hills by William Douglas, The Earl of Angus. After a bloody battle the Scots prevailed, but the losses were great on both sides. One version of the

115

events is that Percy was on a hunting trip and the parcel of land being hunted was known as a chase and since it was in the Cheviots, the name Chevy Chase arises.

In a letter Burns writes "the ballad on Queen Mary was begun while I was busy with Percy's Reliques of English Poetry", providing evidence that he had read the collection and the Ballad of Chevy Chase.

Weel mounted on his grey mare Meg,

From the Ballad of Chevy Chase 50

Sir Hugh Montgomery was he called,
Who, with a spear full bright,
Well mounted on a gallant steed,
Ran fiercely through the fight;

Dougal Graham (1724-1779) the Skellat Bellman (Town Crier) was known as the King of Scottish Chapbook writers. For nearly two hundred years the common folk of Scotland depended for their reading matter on the many thousands of chapbooks and broadsheets that the chapmen carried around among their other goods.

These chapbooks 'cheap books' costing from a farthing to a few pence dealt with a vast range of subjects including humour, religion, witchcraft and even home-made cures and doctoring. Dougal Graham composed and sold whole series of these Chapbooks and they were distributed by the thousand throughout the country. Many of them were coarse and bawdy, in line with the humour of the day, but many others were on serious subjects such as Covenanting martyrs. It is extremely unlikely that Robert Burns would not have read his works especially when consideration of the Merry Muses of Caledonia is taken into account.

Her cutty sark, o' Paisley harn,

Taken from a satirical highland song attributed to Graham 51

A cutty sark of guid harn sheet,

the story of a tale

The Devils Blue Dye

There are two places in the poem (lines 83 and 156) where the poet uses the colour blue ascribed to articles of clothing.

Until the year 1850, all dyes used in the manufacturing of textiles were derived from natural products and sources. As a consequence, the cost of a dye was directly related to the availability of that natural resource. The more expensive the dye, the more fashionable the item.

Blue dye was at that time derived from one source, the Indigo plant. True indigo comes from plants belonging to the legume genus Indigofera, which is a sub-tropical shrub growing to 4-6 feet in height. The leaves contain chemical components capable of producing a fade resistant blue dye.

The species Indigofera tinctoria, native to Asia, has always been the most valuable of the species that were traded. Where the climate did not suit the Indigo plant blue dye was extracted from other plants but these were not as effective or valued.

As a result, Indigo became 'the king of dye' early in history. The role played by India in the production of the dye is acknowledged in the word "indigo" and the ancient Greeks referred to it as 'the Indian dye'. India supplied the dye to most of the known world and there is evidence of indigo use in mummies dating to 3000 years BC.

As was identified by Daniel Defoe, the two things we cannot control are our passions and our fashions. When fashion dictated blue clothing, the best dye available was the rare indigo and hence the cost of blue items was more expensive than other colours.

As we do today with our designer brands, people of the 18th century were equally as fashion conscious. By using blue clothing Burns is most certainly asserting that both Tam, with his bonnet, and himself, with his trousers, enjoyed some of the finer things in life during this period.

It may well be that the reference made in the poem is merely a fashion

117

statement but it could also refer to much more sinister origins which Burns was well aware of, and that would have fitted with the theme of Tam o' Shanter.

During the expansion of European nations into the Far East, indigo was being traded on a grand scale and, during the early 17th century, the 'indigo craze' exploded in Europe, with the populace clambering for indigo dyed products. India was unable to keep up with demand and the European powers were unhappy at the Indian monopoly, so alternative producers had to be sourced.

The problem was that the nature of the plant and the growing conditions required cultivating it. The answer lay in the tropical colonies most European nations had in the New World. The Spanish began growing indigo along the Pacific coast of Central America, eventually extending all the way to Florida. The French, English, Dutch and Danish all followed in West Indies, Louisiana and the Carolinas.

The cultivation of indigo was almost entirely carried out by slave labour, either Native Americans or those imported from Africa. It was calculated in 1761 that a single slave could care for around two acres of indigo per annum, yielding over 160 pounds of product valued at around £13. To place that in context the most Burns ever earned as a farmer was £7 per annum and the poor in Mauchline at that time subsisted on £2 per annum.

The growing and processing of indigo became so profitable it began to replace some of the other less profitable crops and it became absolutely essential to the economies of most European states. In 1756 Voltaire wrote "One hundred thousand slaves work in sugar mills, indigo and cocoa plantations, sacrificing their lives to gratify our newly acquired appetites".

This all resulted in the naming of indigo as the 'Devil's Blue Dye' and this was a well known term in the original 13 colonies of the United States of America.

Burns was considering travelling to Jamaica in 1786, where Indigo

was grown extensively, and would most certainly have known the crops being cultivated on the plantations. The poet was also aware of the effects of the slave trade on the individuals concerned, as is evidenced in his song The Slave's Lament and would have registered the fact that this suffering was to produce the dye for his trousers.

The Art and Music

Sir Malcolm Arnold CBE (1921-2006) is considered one of the towering figures of 20th century music with a remarkable catalogue of major concert works to his credit. He also composed 132 film scores including Bridge Over the River Kwai which won him an Oscar in 1958.

Sir Malcolm regarded Robert Burns as one of the greatest of poets and composed 'The Tam o' Shanter Overture' in 1955. Sir Malcolm expressed the hope that his own enjoyment of Burns' work, which was reflected in his music, would encourage others to read the poet.

Tam o' Shanter Overture was first performed at a Henry Wood Promenade Concert on 17 August 1955 with Sir Malcolm conducting the Royal Philharmonic Orchestra. It was received with tremendous enthusiasm and was the most popular novelty of that seasons' Proms.

The eight minute overture begins slowly with strings, has a melody with a Scottish flavour then builds velocity in accordance with the pace of the poem. As Tam gallops along, brass and drums suddenly lead to string tremolos with the Scottish character of the music evident. As Tam watches the witches dance, a trombone solo almost articulates the words "Weel done cutty sark", leading to a terrific flurry and a sudden end.

A sample of the piece can be found on the Sir Malcolm Arnold website at www.malcolmarnold.co.uk under Multi Media Music Samples.

In so far as art is concerned the poem has inspired both painting and sculpture, and the following list should not be viewed as comprehensive.

A number of collections of paintings have been done by various artists over the years all inspired by the poem.

By far the most well known set of paintings is the 54 created by

Scottish artist Alexander Goudie.

Alexander Goudie (1933-2004) was born in Paisley and is widely acclaimed as one of Scotland's finest figurative painters. As a portrait painter his sitters have included Her Majesty Queen Elizabeth II and Lord McKay of Clashfern.

A Scot first and foremost, Goudie had a fascination throughout his career for Robert Burns great narrative poem Tam o' Shanter and over many years he recreated the poem in paintings, finally finishing the series in 1996, each painting representing a successive stanza in the poem. They were planned for the National Gallery of Scottish Art which stalled leading to the danger of the paintings being sold off individually in 2000. This led to Brian Souter and Tom Hunter intervening with £500,000 to keep the collection together for the benefit of the Scottish people.

The collection now has a permanent home at Rozelle House in Ayr and is displayed on a rota to the public. The paintings also go on tour due to demand elsewhere in the world from Burns appreciation societies. They have also toured in Scotland.

Irvine Burns Club Museum at Wellwood in Irvine also has a collection of Tam o' Shanter paintings by Angus Scott that, whilst not so well known, are worth a visit. Angus Scott was commissioned by Irvine Burns Club in 1975 to paint five scenes from the poem and they hang on the entrance wall. Scott was better known as an illustrator and worked on numerous magazines including Punch.

Also to be found in Wellwood, hanging on the staircase, are a set of six framed wooden carvings depicting scenes from Tam o' Shanter. The detail on these carvings is exquisite and really gives life to the scenes.

A set of ten scenes from the poem have been painted by modern artist Charles Nasmyth and have gone on exhibition at various locations throughout the country. There is a video of the paintings available on the video sharing web site Youtube (www.youtube.com/watch?v=x UpTn7a5bcI) accompanied by a recitation of the poem.

Stewarton artist Craig Campbell has also done a series of paintings on the poem as well as painting the Tam o' Shanter scenes in the Brig O' Doon Hotel, Alloway.

John Faed (1819-1902) from Gatehouse of Fleet also painted scenes from the poem, most famous of which is the dance of witches in the Kirk. Faed was inspired by Burns, Walter Scott and Shakespeare and his paintings reflect this. He also did a painting of The Cotters Saturday Night.

In addition there are numerous sets of cartoons or caricature drawings depicting scenes from the poem in various publications.

James Thom (1802-1850) a stonemason from Tarbolton was commissioned by David Auld, Custodian of Burns Monument in Alloway, to carve a life size figure of Tam o' Shanter in 1828. What resulted are the statues that can be seen at the Monument Gardens today.

The statues were an immediate success and much loved by the Victorians as they seemed so warm and lifelike. So popular in fact that they went on a tour of Britain in the 1830's calling at Edinburgh, Glasgow, Dumfries and London.

James Thom hired an agent to take copies of the statues on tour in America and when the agent failed to send any money back to him, Thom travelled to the United States to resolve the matter. Thom decided to remain in America and continued making copies of the statues and was responsible for much of the fine carving on the outside of Holy Trinity Church in New York City.

·TAM O'SHANTER·

·SOUTER JOHNIE·

Thom Statues Burns Monument Gardens

Anecdotes

One of the most well known anecdotes on the poem in the Ayrshire area is often used to introduce the poem at Burns Suppers, and relates to the need for Tam to concoct the fiction. The story goes that one market day Tam tied Meg to the rail outside the ale-house in High Street and went in for a few drinks. As horse hair was useful for the construction of fishing line, the young men of Ayr would grab a hair from the tail of a horse in passing and as they travelled the length of the street they could collect quite a few to put towards making their line. The wags of Ayr have it that Tam was so long in the pub that, by the time he came out, all the hair was removed from the tail of his poor horse Meg. Rather than confess this to an irate Kate, Tam made up the story of being chased by witches and, as she was a superstitious individual, she swallowed the yarn hook, line and sinker.

There are other versions of the above but all relate that the horse lost its tail hair and Tam made up the story. Where these accounts originate is unknown but it seems an entertaining, if inaccurate, way to introduce the poem.

Another story imparts that Douglas Graham was riding home one night later than normal, having been caught up in a drinking session. Riding alone in a storm of wind and rain and passing over Brown Carrick Hill near to Brig o' Doon, he lost his bonnet in the tempest. The bonnet had contained all the money which he had made that day at Ayr market. To avoid the inevitable scolding that would ensue from his wife when he got home, Douglas concocted the story of witches in Alloway Kirk, which his wife accepted. The following day Graham returned to Brown Carrick to search for his bonnet and cash which, by good fortune, he happened to find near the road.

John 'Jock' Willis was a seasoned sailing ship master who had taken over his father's firm of ship owners in the port of London who became better known as "White Hat Willis" because he always wore a white top hat. Willis wanted to win the annual race to bring home

the new season tea from China, so decided to commission a new clipper to do just that. He turned to Hercules Linton of Dumbarton to design and build a sleek hulled new vessel.

Linton and his company had never tackled a ship of this size before and soon ran into financial difficulties resulting in bankruptcy. William Denny and Brothers took over the contract building a ship of 963 tons which was launched on the River Leven on Monday 22 November 1869. The name given to the ship was one that was to become renowned and loved throughout the seafaring world, Cutty Sark.

Willis was a great fan of Robert Burns so named his ship after the beautiful witch Nannie in Tam o' Shanter. The figurehead is a carving of Nannie in her 'cutty sark' with her left arm outstretched to grasp the tail of the fleeing Meg.

After a life of service as a tea clipper and a training ship, Cutty Sark was berthed at Greenwich where her new trade was tourists. Unfortunately on 21 May 2007 whilst undergoing renovation there was a fire on board causing considerable damage. Luckily much of the fabric of the ship was not on board and she will be repaired to her former glory.

Footnotes

Abbreviations

AC – The Life and Works of Robert Burns by Allan Cunningham

AMB – The Ayrshire Book of Burns Lore by A M Boyle

ATB – Ayrshire in the Time of Burns by Ayrshire Natural History Society edited by John Strawhorn

CR – The Book of Robert Burns by Rev Charles Rogers

CW – Life and Works of Robert Burns By Dr Robert Chambers Edited by William Wallace

DHJS – The Dwelling House of James Shearer by Joseph D Shearer

HH – The Poetry Of Robert Burns Centenary Edition Edited by W E Henley and T F Henderson

JK – The Poems and Songs of Robert Burns by James Kinsley

OR – Quellenstudien Zu Robert Burns 1773-1791 by Otto Ritter

RBJM – A Biography of Robert Burns by James A Mackay

TC – Burns a Study of the Poems and Songs Thomas Crawford

the story of a tale

1	CW Vol III p217	29	JK Vol III p1348
2	AMB p72	30	AC Vol I p249
3	CR Vol II p170	31	OR p218
4	CW Vol III p115	32	TC p222
5	AC Vol I p248	33	OR p218
6	AMB p117	34	JK Vol III p1355
7	DHJS p3-9	35	JK Vol III p1358
8	ATB p212-213	36	JK Vol III p1358
9	ATB p216	37	JK Vol III p1364
10	ATB p58	38	JK Vol III p1356
11	RBJM p57	39	OR p219
12	RBJM p58	40	JK Vol III p1358
13	RBJM p58	41	JK Vol III p1358
14	CW Vol I p48	42	OR p221
15	RBJM p60	43	JK Vol III p1362
16	CR Vol II p239	44	JK Vol III p1356
17	CR Vol II p240	45	OR p219
18	CR Vol II p143	46	OR p219
19	CR Vol II p344	47	JK Vol III p1362
20	CR Vol II p178	48	OR p221
21	CW Vol III p219	49	OR p220
22	JK Vol III p1360	50	OR p220
23	JK Vol III p1356	51	JK Vol III p1363
24	JK Vol III p1358		
25	JK Vol III p1360		
26	JK Vol III p1360		
27	HH Vol I p441		
28	CW Vol III p211		

Kilmarnock Manuscript

(Courtesy of East Ayrshire Council)

Tam o' Shanter. — A tale. —

Printed vol 3. pa 327

When chapmen billies leave the street,
And drouthy neebors, neebors meet;
As market-days are wearing late,
And folk begin to take the gate;
While we sit bousing at the nappy,
And getting fou, & unco happy,
We think na on the lang Scots miles,
The mosses, waters, slaps & styles,
That lie between us & our hame,
Where sits our sulky, sullen dame,
Gathering her brows like gathering storm,
Nursing her wrath to keep it warm. —

This truth fand honest Tam o' Shanter,
As he frae Ayr ae night did canter:
(Auld Ayr, whom ne'er a town surpasses,
For honest Men, & bonnie lasses.)

O Tam! hadst thou but been sae wise,
As taen thy ain wife Kate's advice!
She tauld thee weel thou was a skellum,
A blethering, blustering, drunken blellum:
That frae November till October,
Ae market-day thou was na sober:
That ilka melder, wi' the Miller,
Thou sat as lang as thou had siller:
That every naig was ca'd a shoe on,
The Smith & thee gat roarin fou on:

That at the L——'s house, even on Sunday,
Thou drank wi' Kirkton Jean till Monday.—
She prophesied, that, late or soon,
Thou wad be found, deep drown'd in Doon;
Or catch'd wi' warlocks in the mirk,
By Alloway's auld, haunted Kirk.—

Ah, gentle dames! it gars me greet,
To think how mony counsels sweet,
How mony lengthen'd, sage advices,
The husband frae tha wife despises!

But to our tale: ae market night,
Tam had got planted, unco right,
Fast by an ingle, bleezin finely,
Wi' reaming Swats that drank divinely:
And at his elbow, Souter Johnie,
His ancient, trusty, drouthy crony;
Tam lo'ed him like a very brither,
They had been fou for weeks thegither.—
The night drave on wi' sangs & clatter,
And ay the ale was growing better:
The landlady & Tam grew gracious,
Wi' secret favors, sweet & precious:
The Souter tauld his queerest stories;
The Landlord's laugh was ready chorus.
The storm without might rair & rustle,
Tam did na ~~care~~ min' the storm a whistle.—

130

As bees flee hame wi' lades o' treasure,
The minutes wing'd their way wi' pleasure:
Kings may be blest, but Tam was glorious,
O'er a' the ills o' life victorious!

But Pleasures are like poppies spread,
You seize the flower, its bloom is shed;
Or like the snow falls in the river,
A moment white, then melts for ever;
Or like the Borealis' race,
That flit ere you can point their place;
Or like the rainbow's lovely form,
Evanishing amid the storm.
Nae man can tether Time or Tide,
The hour approaches Tam maun ride;
That hour, o' Night's black arch the key-stane,
That dreary hour Tam mounts his beast in,
And sic a night he took the road in,
As ne'er poor sinner was abroad in.——

The wind blew as 'twould blawn its last,
The rattling showers rose on the blast,
The speedy gleams the darkness swallowed,
Loud, deep, & lang the thunder bellowed:
That night, a child might understand
The deil had business on his hand.——

Weel mounted on his grey meare, Meg,
A better never lifted leg,
Tam skelpit on thro' dub & mire,
Despising wind, & rain, & fire;

Whiles holding fast his gude blue bonnet,
Whiles crooning o'er an auld Scots sonnet,
Whiles glowring round wi' anxious cares,
Lest bogles catch him unawares;
Kirk-Alloway was drawing nigh,
Where ghaists & houlets nightly cry. —

By this time he was cross the ford,
Where in the snaw the chapman smoor'd;
And past the birks, & meikle stane,
Where drunken Charlie brak's neck-bane;
And thro' the whins, & by the cairn,
Where hunters fand the murder'd bairn;
And near the tree, aboon the well,
Where Mungo's mither hang'd hersel. —
Before him Doon pours all his floods,
The doubling storm roars thro' the woods;
The lightenings flash frae pole to pole,
Near, & more near, the thunders roll:
When glimmering thro' the groaning trees,
Kirk-Alloway seem'd in a bleeze,
Thro' ilka bore the beams were glancing,
And loud resounded mirth & dancing. —

Inspiring, bold John Barleycorn!
What dangers thou canst make us scorn!
Wi' tippeny, we fear nae evil;
Wi' usquabae, we'll face the devil!
The swats sae ream'd in Tammie's noddle,
Fair play, he car'd na deils a boddle;
But Maggie stood, right sair astonish'd,
Till, by the heel & hand admonish'd,

She ventur'd forward on the light,
And, wow! Tam saw an unco sight!

Warlocks & witches in a dance,
Nae cotillon brent new frae France,
But hornpipes, jigs, Strathspeys, & reels,
Put life & mettle in their heels: —
A winnock-bunker in the east,
There sat auld Nick in shape o' beast;
A towzie tyke, black, grim, & large,
To gie them music was his charge:
He screw'd the pipes & gart them skirl,
Till roof & rafters a' did dirl. —
~~The torches climb around the wa',~~
~~Infernal fires, blue-bleezing a';~~
By which heroic Tam was able
To note upon the haly table;
A murderer's banes, in gibbet-airns;
Twa span-lang, wee, unchristen'd bairns;
A thief, new-cutted frae a rape,
Wi' his last gasp his gab did gape;
Five tomahawks wi' blude red-rusted;
Five scymitars wi' murder crusted;
~~Seven gallows-pins, three hangman's whittle,~~
~~A~~ ~~wee~~ ~~Doctors' bottles;~~
A garter which a babe had strangled;
A knife a father's throat had mangled,
Whom his ain son of life bereft,
The gray-hairs yet stack to the heft:

[left margin, vertical:] † Confine stood round, like open presses; That shaw'd the Deed in their last dresses; And by some devilish cantraip slight Each in its auld hand held a light.

Th' mair of horrible & awefu',
Which even to name wad be unlawfu'! —
Three Lawyers' tongues, turn'd inside out,
Wi' lies seam'd like a beggar's clout;
Three Priests' hearts, rotten black as muck,
Lay stinking, vile, in every neuk. —

As Tammie glowr'd, amaz'd & curious,
The mirth & fun grew fast & furious;
The Piper loud & louder blew,
The Dancers quick & quicker flew;
They reel'd, they set, they cross'd, they cleekit,
Till ilka Carlin swat & reekit,
And coost her duddies on the wark,
And linket at it in her sark. ——

Now Tam! O Tam! had thae been queans,
A' plump & strappin in their teens!
Their sarks, instead o' creeshie flainen,
Been snaw-white, seventeen-hunder linen;
Thir breeks o' mine, my only pair,
That ance were plush o' gude blue hair,
I wad hae gien them off my hurdies,
For ae blink o' the bonie burdies!
But wither'd beldams, auld & droll,
Rigwoodie hags, wad spean a foal,
Loupin & flingin on a crummock,
I wonder did na turn thy stomach. —

But

134

But Tam kend what was what fu' brawlie;
There was ae winsome wench & walie,
That night enlisted in the core,
(Lang after kend on Carrick-shore;
For mony a beast to dead she shot,
And perish'd mony a bonie boat,
And shook both meikle corn & bear,
And kept the Country-side in fear:)
Her cutty-sark o' Paisley harn,
That while a lassie she had worn,
In longitude tho' sorely scanty,
It was her best, & she was vauntie. —
Ah, little thought thy reverend grannie,
That sark she coft for her wee Nannie,
Wi' twa pund Scots, (twas a' her riches,)
Should ever grac'd a dance o' witches!

But here, my Muse her wing maun cour,
Sic flights are far beyond her power;
To sing, how Nannie lap & flang,
(A souple jad she was, & strang;)
And how Tam stood, like ane bewitch'd,
And thought his very een enrich'd:
Even Satan glowr'd, & fidg'd fu' fain,
And hotch'd, & blew wi' might & main:
Till, first ae caper, syne anither,
Tam lost his reason a' thegither,
And roars out — "Weel done, Cutty-sark!"
And in an instant all was dark:
And scarcely had he Maggie rallied,
When out the hellish legion sallied. —

As bees bizz out, wi' angry fyke,
When plundering herds assail their byke;
As open Pussie's mortal foes,
When, pop, she starts before their nose;
As eager runs the market-croud,
When, "catch the thief!" resounds aloud;
So Maggy runs, the witches follow,
Wi' mony an eldritch skriech & hollow. —

Ah, Tam! Ah, Tam! thou'll get thy fairin!
In hell they'll roast thee like a herrin!
In vain thy Kate awaits thy comin!
Kate soon will be a woefu' woman!
Now, do thy speedy utmost, Meg,
And win the key-stane o' the brig;
There at them thou thy tail may toss,
A running stream they dare na cross:
But ere the key stane she could make,
The fient a tail she had to shake!
For Nannie, far before the rest,
Hard upon noble Maggy prest,
And flew at Tam wi' furious ettle;
But little wist she Maggy's mettle;
Ae spring brought off her master hale,
But left behind her ain grey tail:
The Carlin claught her by the rump,
And left poor Maggie scarce a stump. —

Now, wha this Tale o' truth shall read,
Ilk Man, & Mother's son take heed:

Whene'er to Drink you are inclin'd,
Or Cutty-Sarks rin in your mind,
Think, ye may buy the joys o'er dear,
Remember Tam-o' Shanter's meare. —

Appendix II

Dumfries Competition Winners

(Courtesy of Dumfries Ladies Burns Club)

Year	Winner
1989	Bob Shankland
1990	Jim Brown
1991	Bill Morrison
1992	Jim Brown
1993	Donny McCuaig
1994	Les Byers
1995	William Maxwell
1996	Cameron Goodall
1997	Sophia Harkness
1998	Ronnie Chrichton
1999	Tom McCallum
2000	Fiona Jesseman
2001	Angus Middleton
2002	Matt Muir
2003	Jim Campbell
2004	Ronnie O'Byrne
2005	Jean Wilson
2006	Stewart Moffat
2007	Fiona Jesseman
2008	Willie Horne
2009	Margaret Cook

the story of a tale

Appendix III

Useful Contact Information

Burns National Heritage Park, Murdoch's Lone, Alloway, KA7 4PQ telephone 01292 443700. Web site is www.burnsheritagepark.com and emails to info@burnsheritagepark.com. The Tam o' Shanter Experience is open 7 days April to October 9.30 am – 5.30 pm and November to March 10 am – 5 pm. The centre is closed Christmas Day, Boxing Day and New Years Day. The Monument and Gardens are open seven days April to September 10 am – 5 pm and October to March 10 am – 4 pm and admission is free.

Souter Johnnie's Cottage Main Street, Kirkoswald, KA19 8HY telephone 0844 493 2147. The museum is open April to September on Friday to Tuesday 11.30 am – 5 pm and on 25 January 11.30 am -5 pm. Admission is charged at the National Trust for Scotland Band D rate. Further information on the web site www.nts.org.uk.

Irvine Burns Club, Wellwood, 28 Eglinton Street, Irvine KA12 8AS. Museum opening times are Easter to September Monday/ Wednesday/ Friday/ Saturday 2.30 pm – 4.30 pm and October to March Saturday 2.30 pm – 4.30 pm. Admission is free. Viewing at other times may be arranged in advance with the club secretary by email to info@irvineburnsclub.org.

Cutty Sark is part of the Maritime Greenwich World Heritage site and whilst the current conservation project continues there is no access for visitors. More information can be found at www.cuttysark.org.uk.

Rozelle House Galleries and Maclaurin Galleries are situated in Rozelle Park, Monument Road, Ayr, KA7 4NQ telephone 01292 445447. Entry to the galleries is free and open Monday to Saturday 10 am to 5 pm and on Sundays from April to October from 2 pm to 5 pm. Full details can be found at www.south-ayrshire.gov.uk in the Museums and Galleries section.

Bibliography

A New Map of Ayrshire Comprehending Kyle, Cunninghame and Carrick 1775 by Andrew and Moysten Armstrong

Enemies of God: The Witch-hunt in Scotland by Christina Larner

Witchcraft by James Pennethorne Hughes

Ayrshire at the Time of Burns by Ayrshire Natural History Society edited by John Strawhorn

Who's Who in Burns by John D Ross LLD

Life and Works of Robert Burns (4 Volumes) by Dr Robert Chambers edited by William Wallace

The Poetry of Robert Burns Centenary Edition (4 Volumes) by W.E. Henley and T.F. Henderson

The Poems and Songs of Robert Burns (3 Volumes) by James Kinsley

Robert Burns The Complete Letters by James A Mackay

A Biography of Robert Burns by James A Mackay

Robert Burns The Complete Poetical Works by James A Mackay

Burns A-Z The Complete Word Finder by James A Mackay

Burns a Study of the Poems and Songs by Thomas Crawford

Robert Burns and the Sentimental Era by Carol McGuirk

The Works of Robert Burns (8 Volumes) by Allan Cunningham

Life of Burns by John Gibson Lockhart

The Book of Robert Burns (3 Volumes) by Rev Charles Rogers

Robert Burns by David Daiches

The Dwelling House of James Shearer by Joseph D Shearer

Ayrshire Book of Burns Lore by Andrew M Boyle

A Picture of Scotland Volume 1 by Robert Chambers

God, The Poet & The Devil Robert Burns and Religion by Donald Smith

the story of a tale

Quellenstuden zu Robert Burns 1773-1791 by Otto Ritter

Tales of the Clachan by Rosaleen Murdoch

Rambles in Galloway by Malcolm McLachlan Harper

in and out of Tam o'Shanter

142

the story of a tale